PLEASURE GREEN

MICROSOFT FABRIC: A Comprehensive Beginner's Guide to Leveraging Microsoft Fabric for End-to-End Analytics: Exploring Power BI, Azure Synapse, SQL, and Azure Data

1

INTRODUCTION

Microsoft Fabric is an all-in-one analytics solution for enterprises that covers everything from data movement to data science, Real-Time Analytics, and business intelligence. It offers a comprehensive suite of services, including data lake, data engineering, and data integration, all in one place.

With Fabric, you don't need to piece together different services from multiple vendors. Instead, you can enjoy a highly integrated, end-to-end, and easy-to-use product that is designed to simplify your analytics needs.

The platform is built on a foundation of Software as a Service (SaaS), which takes simplicity and integration to a whole new level.

Microsoft Fabric brings together new and existing components from Power BI, Azure Synapse, and Azure Data Explorer into a single integrated environment. These components are then presented in various customized user experiences.

WHAT IS MICROSOFT FABRIC

Microsoft Fabric is an all-in-one analytics solution for enterprises that covers everything from data movement to data science, Real-Time Analytics, and business intelligence. It offers a comprehensive suite of services, including data lake, data engineering, and data integration, all in one place.

With Fabric, you don't need to piece together different services from multiple vendors. Instead, you can enjoy a highly integrated, end-to-end, and easy-to-use product that is designed to simplify your analytics needs.

The platform is built on a foundation of Software as a Service (SaaS), which takes simplicity and integration to a whole new level.

Microsoft Fabric brings together new and existing components from Power BI, Azure Synapse, and Azure Data Explorer into a single integrated environment. These components are then presented in various customized user experiences.

Fabric brings together experiences such as Data Engineering, Data Factory, Data Science, Data Warehouse, Real-Time Analytics, and Power BI onto a shared SaaS foundation. This integration provides the following advantages:

- An extensive range of deeply integrated analytics in the industry.
- Shared experiences across experiences that are familiar and easy to learn.
- Developers can easily access and reuse all assets.
- A unified data lake that allows you to retain the data where it is while using your preferred analytics tools.
- Centralized administration and governance across all experiences.

With the Microsoft Fabric SaaS experience, all the data and the services are seamlessly integrated. IT teams can centrally configure core enterprise capabilities and permissions are automatically applied across all the underlying services. Additionally, data sensitivity labels are inherited automatically across the items in the suite.

Fabric allows creators to concentrate on producing their best work, freeing them from the need to integrate, manage, or understand the underlying infrastructure that supports the experience.

COMPONENTS OF MICROSOFT FABRIC

Microsoft Fabric offers the comprehensive set of analytics experiences designed to work together seamlessly. Each experience is tailored to a specific persona and a specific task. Fabric includes industry-leading experiences in the following categories for an end-to-end analytical need.

Data Engineering

Data Engineering experience provides a world class Spark platform with great authoring experiences, enabling data engineers to perform large scale data transformation and democratize data through the lakehouse. Microsoft Fabric Spark's integration with Data Factory enables notebooks and spark jobs to be scheduled and orchestrated.

Data Factory

Azure Data Factory combines the simplicity of Power Query with the scale and power of Azure Data Factory. You can use more than 200 native connectors to connect to data sources on-premises and in the cloud.

Data Science

Data Science experience enables you to build, deploy, and operationalize machine learning models seamlessly within your Fabric experience. It integrates with Azure Machine Learning to provide built-in experiment tracking and model registry. Data scientists are empowered to enrich organizational data with predictions and allow business analysts to integrate those predictions into their BI reports. This way it shifts from descriptive to predictive insights.

Data Warehouse

Data Warehouse experience provides industry leading SQL performance and scale. It fully separates compute from storage, enabling independent scaling of both the components. Additionally, it natively stores data in the open Delta Lake format

Real-Time Analytics

Observational data, which is collected from various sources such as apps, IoT devices, human interactions, and so many more. It's currently the fastest growing data category. This data is often semi-structured in formats like JSON or Text. It comes in at high volume, with shifting schemas. These characteristics make it hard for traditional data warehousing platforms to work with. Real-Time Analytics is best in class engine for observational data analytics.

Power BI

Power BI is the world's leading Business Intelligence platform. It ensures that business owners can access all the data in Fabric quickly and intuitively to make better decisions with data.

Fabric brings together all these experiences into a unified platform to offer the most comprehensive big data analytics platform in the industry.

Microsoft Fabric enables organizations, and individuals, to turn large and complex data repositories into actionable workloads and analytics, and is an implementation of data mesh architecture.

ONELAKE AND LAKEHOUSE - THE UNIFICATION OF LAKEHOUSES

The Microsoft Fabric platform unifies the OneLake and lakehouse architecture across the enterprises.

OneLake

The data lake is the foundation on which all the Fabric services are built. Microsoft Fabric Lake is also known as OneLake. It's built into the Fabric service and provides a unified location to store all organizational data where the experiences operate.

OneLake is built on top of ADLS (Azure Data Lake Storage) Gen2. It provides a single SaaS experience and a tenant-wide store for data that serves both professional and citizen developers. The OneLake SaaS experience simplifies the experiences, eliminating the need for users to understand any infrastructure concepts such as resource groups, RBAC (Role-Based Access Control), Azure Resource Manager, redundancy, or regions. Additionally it doesn't require the user to even have an Azure account.

OneLake eliminates today's pervasive and chaotic data silos, which individual developers create when they provision and configure their own isolated storage accounts. Instead, OneLake provides a single, unified storage system for all developers, where discovery and data sharing is trivial and compliance with policy and security settings are enforced centrally and uniformly. For more information, see What is OneLake?

Organizational structure of OneLake and lakehouse

OneLake is hierarchical in nature to simplify management across your organization. It's built into Microsoft Fabric and there's no requirement for any up-front provisioning. There's only one OneLake per tenant and it provides a single-pane-of-glass file-system namespace that spans across users, regions and even clouds. The data in OneLake is divided into manageable containers for easy handling.

The tenant maps to the root of OneLake and is at the top level of the hierarchy. You can create any number of workspaces within a tenant, which can be thought of as folders.

The following image shows the various Fabric items where data is stored. It's an example of how various items within Fabric would store data inside OneLake. As displayed, you can create multiple workspaces within a tenant, create multiple lakehouses within each workspace. A lakehouse is a collection of files, folders, and tables that represents a database over a data lake.

Every developer and business unit in the tenant can instantly create their own workspaces in OneLake. They can ingest data into their own lakehouses, start processing, analyzing, and collaborating on the data, just like OneDrive in Office.

All the Microsoft Fabric compute experiences are prewired to OneLake, just like the Office applications are prewired to use the organizational OneDrive. The experiences such as Data Engineering, Data Warehouse, Data Factory, Power BI, and Real-Time Analytics use OneLake as their native store. They don't need any extra configuration.

OneLake is designed to allow instant mounting of existing PaaS storage accounts into OneLake with the Shortcut feature. There's no need to migrate or move any of the existing data. Using shortcuts, you can access the data stored in Azure Data Lake Storage.

Additionally, shortcuts allow you to easily share data between users and applications without moving or duplicating information. The shortcut capability extends to other storage systems, allowing you to compose and analyze data across clouds with transparent, intelligent caching that reduces egress costs and brings data closer to compute.

ENABLE MICROSOFT FABRIC FOR YOUR ORGANIZATION

You can enable Microsoft Fabric for:

Your tenant - Use this option to be an early adopter of Microsoft Fabric.

A specific capacity - Use this option if you want users in a specific capacity to try out Microsoft Fabric.

In both cases, you can use security groups to provide Microsoft Fabric access to a specified list of users.

Enable for your tenant

When you enable Microsoft Fabric using the tenant setting, users can create Fabric items in that tenant. Depending on the configuration you select, Microsoft Fabric becomes available for everyone in the tenant, or to a selected group of users.

In your tenant, you can enable Microsoft Fabric for:

The entire organization - In most cases your organization has one tenant, so selecting this option enables it for the entire organization. In organizations that have several tenants, if you want to enable Microsoft Fabric for the entire organization, you need to enable it in each tenant.

Specific security groups - Use this option to enable Microsoft Fabric for specific users. You can either specify the security groups that Microsoft Fabric will be enabled for, or the security groups that Microsoft Fabric won't be available for.

STEPS TO ENABLE MICROSOFT FABRIC FOR YOUR TENANT.

- Navigate to the tenant settings in the admin portal and in Microsoft Fabric (Preview), expand the Users can create Fabric items (public preview).

- Uncheck the Accept Microsoft's default selection (Off for the entire organization) checkbox. You only need to uncheck the Microsoft's default selection when you enable the Microsoft Fabric setting for the first time.

- Enable the Users can create Fabric items (public preview) switch.

- (Optional) Use the Specific security groups option to enable Microsoft Fabric for specific users. You can also use the Except specific security groups option, to enable Microsoft Fabric for the tenant, and exclude specific users.

24

- Select Apply.

ENABLE FOR A CAPACITY

Consider the Microsoft Fabric setting a recommendation for the entire organization. Capacity admins can override this setting, depending on their needs. For example, because Microsoft Fabric is a preview product, your organization decided not to enable it. However, your organization also has a group of highly advanced developers who want to experiment with Microsoft Fabric. In such cases, Microsoft Fabric can be enabled at the capacity level.

STEPS TO ENABLE MICROSOFT FABRIC FOR A SPECIFIC CAPACITY

- Navigate to the capacity settings in the admin portal.
- Select the capacity you want to enable Microsoft Fabric for.
- Select the Delegate tenant settings tab, and under Microsoft Fabric (Preview), expand the Users can create Fabric items (public preview) setting.
- Check the Override tenant admin selection checkbox and verify that the Users can create Fabric items (public preview) setting is enabled.

- (Optional) Use the Specific security groups option to enable Microsoft Fabric for specific users. You can also use the Except specific security groups option, to enable Microsoft Fabric for the capacity, and exclude specific users.

- Select Apply.

CAN I DISABLE MICROSOFT FABRIC?

To disable Microsoft Fabric, you can turn off the Microsoft Fabric (Preview) admin switch. After disabling Microsoft Fabric, users will have view permissions for Microsoft Fabric items. If you disable Microsoft Fabric for a specific capacity while Microsoft Fabric is available in your organization, your selection will only affect that capacity.

Considerations

In some cases, users that don't have Microsoft Fabric enabled will be able to view Microsoft Fabric items and icons.

Users that don't have Microsoft Fabric enabled, can:

- View Microsoft Fabric items created by other users in the same workspace, as long as they have at least read-only access to that workspace.

- View Microsoft Fabric icons in capacities where other users have Microsoft Fabric enabled, as long as they have at least read-only access to that capacity.

FABRIC IS A COMPLETE ANALYTICS PLATFORM

Every analytics project has multiple subsystems. Every subsystem needs a different array of capabilities, often requiring products from multiple vendors. Integrating these products can be a complex, fragile, and expensive endeavor.

With Fabric, customers can use a single product with a unified experience and architecture that provides all the capabilities required for a developer to extract insights from data and present it to the business user. And by delivering the experience as software as a service (SaaS), everything is automatically integrated and optimized, and users can sign up within seconds and get real business value within minutes.

Fabric empowers every team in the analytics process with the role-specific experiences they need, so data engineers, data warehousing professionals, data scientists, data analysts, and business users feel right at home.

Fabric comes with seven core workloads:

- Data Factory (preview) provides more than 150 connectors to cloud and on-premises data sources, drag-

and-drop experiences for data transformation, and the ability to orchestrate data pipelines.

- Synapse Data Engineering (preview) enables great authoring experiences for Spark, instant start with live pools, and the ability to collaborate.

- Synapse Data Science (preview) provides an end-to-end workflow for data scientists to build sophisticated AI models, collaborate easily, and train, deploy, and manage machine learning models.

- Synapse Data Warehousing (preview) provides a converged lake house and data warehouse experience with industry-leading SQL performance on open data formats.

- Synapse Real-Time Analytics (preview) enables developers to work with data streaming in from the Internet of Things (IoT) devices, telemetry, logs, and more, and analyze massive volumes of semi-structured data with high performance and low latency.

- Power BI in Fabric provides industry-leading visualization and AI-driven analytics that enable business analysts and business users to gain insights from data. The Power BI experience is also deeply integrated into Microsoft 365, providing relevant insights where business users already work.

29

- Data Activator (coming soon) provides real-time detection and monitoring of data and can trigger notifications and actions when it finds specified patterns in data—all in a no-code experience.

FABRIC IS LAKE-CENTRIC AND OPEN

Today's data lakes can be messy and complicated, making it hard for customers to create, integrate, manage, and operate data lakes. And once they are operational, multiple data products using different proprietary data formats on the same data lake can cause significant data duplication and concerns about vendor lock-in.

STORAGE: ONELAKE

OneLake is a Data Lake technology that emphasizes being the ONE data lake. This will be the storage for all the computing services mentioned above. They will all store data in the OneLake and read it from there. The idea behind using a Data Lake technology is that it would cover both types of structured and unstructured data. OneLake will automatically cover the regions through one tenant, so there won't be a need to create a data lake for each region. One Data Lake would be enough for all, hence the OneLake.

DATA INTEGRATION: AZURE DATA FACTORY AND DATAFLOW

Microsoft has invested a long time in data integration technologies. Azure Data Factory is the successor technology of SSIS (SQL Server Integration Services). Azure Data Factory has the power to transfer billions and trillions of rows of data. Recent enhancements in Power Query technology also bring Dataflow as the transformation engine that can now be used alongside Data Factory for a comprehensive Data Integration technology. Azure Data Factory is the ETL technology for a data professional, whereas Dataflow and Power Query are usually the technology for the Data Analyst. In Trident, the experience of Data Integration would use the best of both worlds and will give you the scalability and the transformation power in one place.

DATA ENGINEERING: SYNAPSE

For data engineers, Synapse provides the ability to build the infrastructure using Lakehouse (OneLake) and then pipelines to ingest the data into that structure. There will be connectors for various data sources, and the data will be stored in the Lakehouse as files or data tables, depending on the source type. The data can be moved into the Lakehouse using Shortcuts or Data integration methods mentioned in the previous section.

The Lakehouse is not just for storing the data but also for table management. Synapse helps you to have better performance and management across the Lakehouse.

DATA WAREHOUSING: SYNAPSE

When you work with a large-scale data warehouse, Synapse gives you immense power to manage that. You can query the data with an amazing, empowered performance using SQL technology combined with Apache Spark for big data. Azure Data Explorer (Kusto) can be used for interacting with this technology, and with the Fabric, now Kusto is part of the overall experience. You won't need to use a separate tool or editor for it.

Synapse provides an open and infinitely scalable data warehouse. As the data warehouse developer or admin, you don't have to worry about providing more resources to scale up or down. Everything will be done for you automatically. Data is stored in an open format parquet file. The difference between Synapse Data Warehouse with creating Data Warehouse in Azure SQL DB, or even using Dataflow is that Synapse is enterprise-ready and infinitely scalable.

DATA SCIENCE: SYNAPSE

Data Science projects are usually part of the bigger data analytics work. That is why in Microsoft Fabric, Data Science using Synapse is added as a workload. Data Science is not just using a single tool; it is a combination of features and tools used across the entire Microsoft Fabric. The process can include using analyzing the data using Data Wrangler, building models and experiments using MLFlow, model training, usage of Cognitive Services and large language models, and prediction using PREDICT. Synapse ML would be supporting all these in Microsoft Fabric.

REALTIME ANALYTICS: SYNAPSE

The ability to analyze real-time data using IOT Analytics and Log Analytics has been part of Microsoft's offering for a long time. This ability is now part of the Microsoft Fabric as Synapse Real-time Analytics workload. Synapse Real-time Analytics works with event streaming technologies (such as IoT or Event Hubs, pipelines, etc.), loading data into KQL DB and Lakehouse via mirroring and then ML models to run experiments on it, and finally, use Power BI to see the results.

WHAT IS POWER BI?

Power BI is a collection of software services, apps, and connectors that work together to turn your unrelated sources of data into coherent, visually immersive, and interactive insights. Your data might be an Excel spreadsheet, or a collection of cloud-based and on-premises hybrid data warehouses. Power BI lets you easily connect to your data sources, visualize and discover what's important, and share that with anyone or everyone you want.

THE PARTS OF POWER BI

Power BI consists of several elements that all work together, starting with these three basics:

- A Windows desktop application called Power BI Desktop.
- An online software as a service (SaaS) service called the Power BI service.
- Power BI Mobile apps for Windows, iOS, and Android devices.

These three elements—Power BI Desktop, the service, and the mobile apps—are designed to let you create, share, and consume business insights in the way that serves you and your role most effectively.

Beyond those three, Power BI also features two other elements:

- Power BI Report Builder, for creating paginated reports to share in the Power BI service. Read more about paginated reports later in this article.

- Power BI Report Server, an on-premises report server where you can publish your Power BI reports, after creating them in Power BI Desktop.

HOW POWER BI MATCHES YOUR ROLE

How you use Power BI depends on your role in a project or on a team. Other people, in other roles, might use Power BI differently.

For example, you might primarily use the Power BI service to view reports and dashboards. Your number-crunching, business-report-creating coworker might make extensive use of Power BI Desktop or Power BI Report Builder to create reports, then publish those reports to the Power BI service, where you view them. Another coworker, in sales, might mainly use the Power BI Mobile app to monitor progress on sales quotas, and to drill into new sales lead details.

If you're a developer, you might use Power BI APIs to push data into datasets or to embed dashboards and reports into your own custom applications. Have an idea for a new visual? Build it yourself and share it with others.

You also might use each element of Power BI at different times, depending on what you're trying to achieve or your role for a given project.

How you use Power BI can be based on which feature or service of Power BI is the best tool for your situation. For example, you can use Power BI Desktop to create reports for your own team about customer engagement statistics and you can view inventory and manufacturing progress in a real-time dashboard in the Power BI service. You can create a paginated report of mailable invoices, based on a Power BI dataset. Each part of Power BI is available to you, which is why it's so flexible and compelling.

Explore documents that pertain to your role:

- Power BI for business users
- Power BI Desktop for report creators
- Power BI Report Builder for enterprise report creators
- Power BI for administrators
- Power BI for developers

THE FLOW OF WORK IN POWER BI

One common workflow in Power BI begins by connecting to data sources in Power BI Desktop and building a report. You then publish that report from Power BI Desktop to the Power BI service, and share it so business users in the Power BI service and on mobile devices can view and interact with the report.

USE THE DEPLOYMENT PIPELINE TOOL

In the Power BI service, you can use the deployment pipeline tool to test your content before you release it to your users. The deployment pipeline tool can help you deploy reports, dashboards, datasets, and paginated reports. Read about how to get started with deployment pipelines in the Power BI service.

PAGINATED REPORTS IN THE POWER BI SERVICE

Another workflow involves paginated reports in the Power BI service. Enterprise report creators design paginated reports to be printed or shared. They can also share these reports in the Power BI service. They're called paginated because they're formatted to fit well on a page. They're often used for operational reports, or for printing forms such as invoices or transcripts. They display all the data in a table, even if the table spans multiple pages. Power

BI Report Builder is the standalone tool for authoring paginated reports.

AZURE AND POWER BI

With Azure services and Power BI, you can turn your data processing efforts into analytics and reports that provide real-time insights into your business. Whether your data processing is cloud-based or on-premises, straightforward, or complex, single-sourced or massively scaled, warehoused, or real-time, Azure and Power BI have the built-in connectivity and integration to bring your business intelligence efforts to life.

Power BI has a multitude of Azure connections available, and the business intelligence solutions you can create with those services are as unique as your business. You can connect as few as one Azure data source, or a handful, then shape and refine your data to build customized reports.

AZURE SQL DATABASE AND POWER BI

You can start with a straightforward connection to an Azure SQL Database, and create reports to monitor the progress of your business. Using the Power BI Desktop, you can create reports that identify trends and key performance indicators that move your business forward.

TRANSFORM, SHAPE, AND MERGE YOUR CLOUD DATA

Do you have more complex data, and all sorts of sources? No problem. With Power BI Desktop and Azure services, connections are just a tap of the Get Data dialog away. Within the same query you can connect to your Azure SQL Database, your Azure HDInsight data source, and your Azure Blob Storage or Azure Table Storage. Then select only the subsets within each that you need, and refine it from there.

You can create different reports for different audiences too, using the same data connections and even the same query. Just build a new report page, refine your visualizations for each audience, and watch it keep the business in the know.

GET COMPLEX (AND AHEAD) USING AZURE SERVICES AND POWER BI

You can expand as much as you need with Azure and Power BI. Harness multi-source data processing, make use of massive real-time systems, use Stream Analytics and Event Hubs, and coalesce your varied SaaS services into business intelligence reports that give your business an edge.

CONTEXT INSIGHTS WITH POWER BI EMBEDDED ANALYTICS

Embed stunning, interactive data visualizations in applications, websites, portals, and more, to take advantage of your business data. With Power BI Embedded as a resource in Azure, you can easily embed interactive reports and dashboards, so your users can enjoy consistent, high-fidelity experiences across devices. Power BI used with embedding analytics is to help you through your journey from Data to Knowledge to Insights to Actions. Furthermore, you can extend the value of Power BI and Azure also by embedding analytics in your organization's internal applications and portals

EMBED YOUR POWER BI DATA WITHIN YOUR APP

Embed stunning, interactive data visualizations in applications, websites, portals, and more, to showcase your business data in context. Using Power BI Embedded in Azure, you can easily embed interactive reports and dashboards, so your users can enjoy consistent, high-fidelity experiences across devices.

WHAT COULD YOU DO WITH AZURE AND POWER BI?

There are all sorts of scenarios where Azure and Power BI can be combined. The possibilities and opportunities are as unique as your business. For more information about Azure services, check out this overview page, which describes Data Analytics Scenarios using Azure, and learn how to transform your data sources into intelligence that drives your business ahead.

ON-PREMISES REPORTING WITH POWER BI REPORT SERVER

What if you need to keep your reports on premises, say, behind a firewall?

You can create, deploy, and manage Power BI reports in Power BI Desktop, and paginated reports in Report Builder, with the ready-to-use tools and services that Power BI Report Server provides.

OPEN DATA FORMATS ACROSS ANALYTICS OFFERINGS

Fabric is deeply committed to open data formats across all its workloads and tiers. Fabric treats Delta on top of Parquet files as a native data format that is the default for all workloads. This deep commitment to a common open data format means that customers need to load the data into the lake only once and all the workloads can operate on the same data, without having to separately ingest it. It also means that OneLake supports structured data of any format and unstructured data, giving customers total flexibility.

By adopting OneLake as our store and Delta and Parquet as the common format for all workloads, we offer customers a data stack that's unified at the most fundamental level. Customers do not need to maintain different copies of data for databases, data lakes, data warehousing, business intelligence, or real-time analytics. Instead, a single copy of the data in OneLake can directly power all the workloads.

Managing data security (table, column, and row levels) across different data engines can be a persistent nightmare for customers. Fabric will provide a universal security model that is managed in OneLake, and all engines enforce it uniformly as they process queries and jobs. This model is coming soon.

FABRIC IS POWERED BY AI

We are infusing Fabric with Azure OpenAI Service at every layer to help customers unlock the full potential of their data, enabling developers to leverage the power of generative AI against their data and assisting business users to find insights in their data. With Copilot in Microsoft Fabric in every data experience, users can use conversational language to create dataflows and data pipelines, generate code and entire functions, build machine learning models, or visualize results. Customers can even create their own conversational language experiences that combine Azure OpenAI Service models and their data and publish them as plug-ins.

Copilot in Microsoft Fabric builds on our existing commitments to data security and privacy in the enterprise. Copilot inherits an organization's security, compliance, and privacy policies. Microsoft does not use organizations' tenant data to train the base language models that power Copilot.

Copilot in Microsoft Fabric will be coming soon. Stay tuned to the Microsoft Fabric blog for the latest updates and public release date for Copilot in Microsoft Fabric.

WHAT IS DATA FACTORY IN MICROSOFT FABRIC?

Data Factory empowers you with a modern data integration experience to ingest, prepare and transform data from a rich set of data sources (for example, databases, data warehouse, Lakehouse, real-time data, and more). Whether you are a citizen or professional developer, you will be able to transform the data with intelligent transformations and leverage a rich set of activities. With Data Factory in Microsoft Fabric, we are bringing fast copy (data movement) capabilities to both dataflows and data pipelines. With Fast Copy, you can move data between your favorite data stores blazing fast. Most importantly, Fast Copy enables you to bring data to your Lakehouse and Data Warehouse in Microsoft Fabric for analytics.

There are two primary high-level features Data Factory implements: dataflows and pipelines.

- Dataflows enable you to leverage more than 300 transformations in the dataflows designer, letting you transform data easier and with more flexibility than any other tool - including smart AI-based data transformations.

- Data pipelines enable you to leverage the out-of-the-box rich data orchestration capabilities to compose flexible data workflows that meet your enterprise needs.

DATAFLOWS

Dataflows provide a low-code interface for ingesting data from hundreds of data sources, transforming your data using 300+ data transformations. You can then load the resulting data into multiple destinations, such as Azure SQL databases and more. Dataflows can be run repeatedly using manual or scheduled refresh, or as part of a data pipeline orchestration.

Dataflows are built using the familiar Power Query experience that's available today across several Microsoft products and services such as Excel, Power BI, Power Platform, Dynamics 365 Insights applications, and more. Power Query empowers all users, ranging from citizen to pro, to perform data ingestion and data transformations across their data estate. Perform joins, aggregations, data cleansing, custom transformations, and much more all from an easy-to-use, highly visual, low-code UI.

DATA PIPELINES

Data pipelines enable powerful workflow capabilities at cloud-scale. With data pipelines, you can build complex workflows that can refresh your dataflow, move PB-size data, and define sophisticated control flow pipelines.

Use data pipelines to build complex ETL and data factory workflows that can perform many different tasks at scale. Control flow capabilities are built into data pipelines that allow you to build workflow logic, which provides loops and conditionals.

Add a configuration-driven copy activity together with your low-code dataflow refresh in a single pipeline for an end-to-end ETL data pipeline. You can even add code-first activities for Spark Notebooks, SQL scripts, stored procs, and more.

MICROSOFT FABRIC- FOR SIMPLICITY

The best way to understand Fabric is to understand its primary purpose; Simplicity. Microsoft team invested in this new offering in the past two years and devised a way to simplify things. As the Data Analytics Lead of your organization, you don't have to worry much about the technology; you can instead focus on the results. You don't have to spend hours and hours to figure out how the licensing of your Azure Synapse combined with Azure Data Factory and Power BI would work together. Fabric makes it much simpler.

MICROSOFT FABRIC- AN UMBRELLA

I like the Umbrella concept. Microsoft did it once in 2015 by bringing Power View, Power Query, and Power Pivot under an umbrella called Power BI. Power BI was a huge success in a way that in the past few years, Power BI always has been on the top of Gartner's Magic Quadrant for BI services in the world.

Fabric is the Data Platform service offering of Microsoft for this new age. Fabric is an umbrella on top of Microsoft's three main Data Analytics products: Power BI, Azure Data Factory, and Azure Synapse. However, it is easier to understand if you look at it by functionality or workload.

FABRIC EMPOWERS EVERY BUSINESS USER

Customers aspire to drive a data culture where everyone in their organization is making better decisions based on data. To help our customers foster this culture, Fabric deeply integrates with the Microsoft 365 applications people use every day.

Power BI is a core part of Fabric and is already infused across Microsoft 365. Through Power BI's deep integrations with popular applications such as Excel, Microsoft Teams, PowerPoint, and SharePoint, relevant data from OneLake is easily discoverable and accessible to users right from Microsoft 365—helping customers drive more value from their data

With Fabric, you can turn your Microsoft 365 apps into hubs for uncovering and applying insights. For example, users in Microsoft Excel can directly discover and analyze data in OneLake and generate a Power BI report with a click of a button. In Teams, users can infuse data into their everyday work with embedded channels, chat, and meeting experiences. Business users can bring data into their presentations by embedding live Power BI reports directly in Microsoft PowerPoint. Power BI is also natively integrated with SharePoint, enabling easy sharing and dissemination of insights. And with Microsoft Graph Data

Connect (preview), Microsoft 365 data is natively integrated into OneLake so customers can unlock insights on their customer relationships, business processes, security and compliance, and people productivity.

FABRIC REDUCES COSTS THROUGH UNIFIED CAPACITIES

Today's analytics systems typically combine products from multiple vendors in a single project. This results in computing capacity provisioned in multiple systems like data integration, data engineering, data warehousing, and business intelligence. When one of the systems is idle, its capacity cannot be used by another system causing significant wastage.

Purchasing and managing resources is massively simplified with Fabric. Customers can purchase a single pool of computing that powers all Fabric workloads. With this all-inclusive approach, customers can create solutions that leverage all workloads freely without any friction in their experience or commerce. The universal compute capacities significantly reduce costs, as any unused compute capacity in one workload can be utilized by any of the workloads.

STREAMLINING DATA ANALYTICS

Data analytics projects involve multiple components, including data visualization, modelling, storage, machine learning, and data transformations. Traditionally, data analytics professionals had to navigate through a myriad of tools and services, each with its own licensing complexities. With Microsoft Fabric, this complexity is alleviated, allowing users to focus more on their analytics work and less on the technical details.

THE KEY COMPONENTS OF MICROSOFT FABRIC

Microsoft Fabric acts as an umbrella over three main tools and services: Azure Synapse, Power BI, and Azure Data Factory. These components offer distinct functionalities, including data integration, engineering, warehousing, science, real-time analytics, and business intelligence. By combining these services under one platform, Microsoft Fabric provides a unified environment for data analytics professionals to build robust and scalable projects.

THE ROLE OF ONE LAKE

At the heart of Microsoft Fabric lies "One Lake," a next-generation storage system for data lakes. Unlike traditional data lake architectures where organizations build separate data lakes for different domains or regions, One Lake offers a centralized and logical layer. This ensures that all data is stored in one location, simplifying data access and management for various services like Power BI, Azure Data Factory, and Azure Synapse.

ADVANTAGES OF MICROSOFT FABRIC

Microsoft Fabric offers several advantages for data analytics professionals. First, it streamlines the analytics process by eliminating the need to navigate through multiple tools and services. Instead, users can leverage the integrated environment of Fabric to access and utilize the necessary components seamlessly. Additionally, Fabric reduces licensing complexities, enabling users to focus more on their analytics goals rather than licensing intricacies.

THE POWER OF INTEGRATION

By integrating tools like Azure Synapse, Power BI, and Azure Data Factory, Microsoft Fabric empowers data analytics professionals to efficiently work on data integration, engineering, warehousing, science, real-time analytics, and business intelligence. The integration fosters collaboration, improves productivity, and enables data-driven decision-making across the organization.

WHAT HAPPENS TO CURRENT MICROSOFT ANALYTICS SOLUTIONS

Existing Microsoft products such as Azure Synapse Analytics, Azure Data Factory, and Azure Data Explorer will continue to provide a robust, enterprise-grade platform as a service (PaaS) solution for data analytics. Fabric represents an evolution of those offerings in the form of a simplified SaaS solution that can connect to existing PaaS offerings. Customers will be able to upgrade from their current products into Fabric at their own pace.

GET STARTED WITH MICROSOFT FABRIC

Microsoft Fabric is currently in preview. Try out everything Fabric has to offer by signing up for the free trial—no credit card information is required. Everyone who signs up gets a fixed Fabric trial capacity, which may be used for any feature or capability from integrating data to creating machine learning models. Existing Power BI Premium customers can simply turn on Fabric through the Power BI admin portal. After July 1, 2023, Fabric will be enabled for all Power BI tenants.

DATA FACTORY IN MICROSOFT FABRIC

As organizations work through their digital transformation journeys, they are awash with data that they need to bring together to meet their analytics needs. To do this, they need to seamlessly access data from a diverse set of data sources, reshape and transform the data to the right format, and load the data into a data store like a lakehouse or data warehouse, where the data can support their analytics needs. In addition, companies are looking to stitch together different data activities (e.g., running a notebook, a stored procedure, SQL script, and more) and orchestrate specific data workflows.

Today, we are unveiling Data Factory in Microsoft Fabric, bringing together the best of Power Query and Azure Data Factory into a single, modern data integration experience which empowers both data and business professionals with capabilities to ingest and transform data as well as orchestrate data workflows. Our goal is to empower everyone to be able to connect to diverse data sources and bring that data to where it can best help you derive insights for better business decisions.

Whether you're a citizen or professional developer, Data Factory enables you to develop enterprise-scale data integration solutions with next-generation dataflows and data pipelines.

Data Factory in Fabric empowers you with:

- Seamless connectivity to more than 170+ data stores (including on-premises data sources, cloud databases, analytical platforms, line of business applications, and more)

- Next-generation Power BI dataflows is now available as part of Data Factory in Fabric, providing 300+ out-of-the box data transformations, including AI transformations, and scalable data flows that run on Fabric compute. In addition, you can output the transformed data into various data destinations.

- Data pipelines in Fabric is an evolution of Azure Data Factory pipelines which provides you with a rich set of integration capabilities. In addition, the copy assistant enables you to jumpstart any copy task from data sources to data destinations.

- Built-in AI enables you to accelerate and automate common data integration tasks.

For example, you might need to extract data from an unstructured data source like a web page or a text file without a well-defined format. With the help of AI, you can now use Data Factory to analyze examples you give on values you want to extract. Then, the powerful AI capabilities underneath the hood learn from the examples and create the Data Factory dataflows to extract just the data you need.

HITACHI SOLUTIONS

Hitachi Solutions provides consulting services to help customers migrate their data systems into Microsoft Fabric. Their global team of IT professionals has extensive expertise using Data Factory in Fabric to seamlessly integrate data from multiple sources.

"The Data Factory experience in Microsoft Fabric has surpassed our data and analytics needs by equipping our customers with industry-leading data orchestration capabilities in an elegant, easy-to-use, code-free experience."

DELPHIX

Delphix has a strong track record of delivering powerful data compliance capabilities to enterprises across industries to address their privacy mandates and cybersecurity requirements. Delphix is partnering with Microsoft to bring their proven technology to the Microsoft Fabric platform with Delphix Compliance Services for Data Factory.

"In collaborating with Microsoft to bring our multi-cloud data masking solution to Microsoft Fabric, Delphix is proud to deliver a comprehensive way to de-risk the cloud while accelerating the path from data to transformation."

GET STARTED WITH MICROSOFT FABRIC

Microsoft Fabric is currently in preview. Try out everything Fabric has to offer by signing up for the free trial—no credit card information required. Everyone who signs up gets a fixed Fabric trial capacity, which may be used for any feature or capability from integrating data to creating machine learning models. Existing Power BI Premium customers can simply turn on Fabric through the Power BI admin portal. After July 1, 2023, Fabric will be enabled by default for all Power BI tenants.

SYNAPSE DATA ENGINEERING IN MICROSOFT FABRIC

Data engineering is playing an increasingly foundational role in every organization's analytics journey. The amount of data that needs to be processed is growing faster than ever, ranging from tabular data to unstructured documents, images, IoT sensors and more. All this data needs to be ingested, processed at scale, and shared with the business. Data engineers need to tackle numerous challenges including data consolidation, security considerations as well as democratization of data, catering to different consumption needs. These processes are complex – data is fragmented across many sources, data sharing requires ETL jobs and synchronization, often to proprietary stores, security needs to be replicated multiple times, leading to inconsistencies. This results in friction and project roadblocks, hampering productivity and leading to frustration.

Today, we are excited to announce the preview of Synapse Data Engineering, one of the core experiences of Microsoft Fabric. Microsoft Fabric empowers teams of data professionals to seamlessly collaborate, end-to-end on their analytics projects, ranging from data integration to data warehousing, data science and business intelligence. With data engineering as a core experience in Fabric, data engineers will feel right at home, being able to leverage the power of Apache Spark to transform their data at scale and build out a robust lakehouse architecture.

WHAT'S INCLUDED IN SYNAPSE DATA ENGINEERING

With Synapse Data Engineering, we aspire to streamline the process of working with your organizational data. Instead of wasting cycles on the 'integration tax' of wiring together a collection of products, worrying about spinning up and managing infrastructure and stitching together disparate data sources, we want data engineers to focus on the jobs to be done.

Here are some of the key Synapse Data Engineering experiences that are launching as part of Microsoft Fabric at Build:

BUILD A LAKEHOUSE FOR ALL YOUR ORGANIZATIONAL DATA

The Synapse Data Engineering lakehouse combines the best of the data lake and warehouse, removing the friction of ingesting, transforming, and sharing organizational data, all in an open format. By making the lakehouse a first-class item in the workspace, we have made it really easy for any data engineer to create it and work with it.

Users can choose from various ways of bringing data into the lakehouse including dataflow & pipelines, and they can even use shortcuts to create virtual folders and tables without the data ever leaving their storage accounts. Ingested data comes by default in the Delta lake format, and tables are automatically created for users.

The lakehouse also streamlines the process of collaborating on top of the same data. Since all the data in Microsoft Fabric is automatically stored in the Delta format, different data professionals can easily work together. The lakehouse comes with a SQL endpoint that provides data warehousing capabilities, including the ability to run T-SQL queries, create views and define functions. Every lakehouse also comes with a semantic dataset, enabling BI users to build reports directly on top of lakehouse data. Power BI can connect to the lakehouse data using 'Direct Lake' mode meaning it can read the data in the lake, with no data movement and with great performance.

RUNTIME WITH GREAT DEFAULT PERFORMANCE & ROBUST ADMIN CONTROLS

We are excited to announce that the Synapse Data Engineering public preview is shipping with 'Runtime 1.1' which includes Spark 3.3.1, Delta 2.2 and Python 3.10. To remove friction in getting started, the Spark Runtime comes pre-wired to every Microsoft Fabric workspace.

In Microsoft Fabric, we strive to provide users with great, out of the box performance, with no tuning required, and Spark is no exception. There are a variety of optimizations built into the runtime to ensure data engineers always have a performant experience. These include Spark query optimizations like partition caching, but also Delta optimizations such as 'V-order'. All Microsoft Fabric engines automatically write Delta with V-order, meaning data is automatically optimized for BI reporting, resulting in great query performance when using Power BI.

We are also committed to amazing start up time performance. In Microsoft Fabric, every workspace comes with a Spark 'starter pool' with default configurations. These pools are kept 'live' meaning Spark sessions now start within 5-15 seconds from the moment you run your notebook, at no additional cost.

Whilst out of the box experiences are key, we realize admins require more granular controls when managing their Spark workload. We are therefore giving admins the ability to create their own custom Spark pools where they can configure parameters like node size, number of nodes, executors and autoscale.

We are also excited to announce that Spark pools will start all the way from a single node, which is a great cost-effective option for test runs or lightweight workloads.

Admins will also be able to install public and custom libraries to the workspace pool, as well as set the default runtime and configure Spark properties. All notebooks & Spark Jobs will inherit the runtime, libraries, & settings without needing to manage things on an artifact-by-artifact basis.

DEVELOPER EXPERIENCE

Our goal is for every data engineer to have a delightful authoring experience, irrespective of their tooling of choice.

The primary authoring canvas offered in Synapse Data Engineering is the notebook. The notebook provides developers with native lakehouse integration, users can easily collaborate thanks to built-in co-authoring, whilst the notebook auto saves, just like in Microsoft Office. Notebooks can be scheduled or added to pipelines for more complex workflows.

Data engineers who want to make use of ad hoc libraries during their session, can install popular Python and R libraries in-line leveraging commands like pip install. Notebooks can also reference each other for more modularized ways of working.

Users who on the other hand prefer low-code experiences can also leverage Data Wrangler, a UI data prep experience built on top of pandas dataframes. Low code operations are automatically translated to code for transparency and reusability.

Notebooks provide fully integrated Spark monitoring experiences inside the notebook cells. The built-in Spark advisor, analyzes Spark executions, and provides users with real-time advice and guidance.

Users can also navigate to the full-blown monitoring hub where they can monitor all current & past Spark jobs, in addition to other Fabric items. They can drill down into job details, view associated notebooks & pipelines, explore notebook snapshots, and navigate to the Spark UI & history server.

We know many developers prefer working in IDEs and so we are also thrilled to announce native VS Code integration with Fabric code artifacts. The Synapse VS Code extension enables users to work with their notebooks, Spark Jobs and lakehouses straight from VS Code. Users can benefit from full debugging support whilst using the Spark clusters in their workspace.

Finally, users who prefer to work in their own environment can leverage the Spark Job Definition (SJD) in Microsoft Fabric. Using the SJD, users can upload their existing JAR files, tweak Spark configurations, add lakehouse reference and submit their jobs. Just like notebooks, SJDs come with monitoring, scheduling and pipeline integration.

COMING SOON

In addition to what is shipping at Microsoft Build, we also have a whole variety of capabilities that are releasing in the coming months. Stay tuned for our monthly blog updates, where we will be keeping you posted on what is newly available.

TOP 10 THINGS TO LOOK FORWARD TO

Lakehouse sharing

End users who want to use the lakehouse for reporting or data science, will be able to easily discover all the lakehouses they have been given access to inside the OneLake Data Hub, the Microsoft Fabric data discovery portal.

Lakehouse security

With 'One Security', table and folder security are applied once inside the lakehouse and is automatically kept in sync across all engines and even external services. This ensures that your data is protected at all times, in a consistent and reliable way.

Spark Autotune

Autotune uses machine learning to analyze previous Spark job runs and tunes the configurations to automatically optimize performance for users.

High Concurrency Mode

Customers will be able to share their notebook sessions, further improving start up times for notebooks attached to existing sessions (as well as reducing costs).

Custom live pools

Users will be able to keep their custom pools 'live' meaning these will also be able to benefit from the fast start up times (like starter pools).

Environments

To give users more flexibility when managing their Spark workload, they will be able to configure an 'environment'. Inside they can select their Spark pool, default runtime and install libraries. Environments can be attached to notebooks and Spark jobs, overriding the default.

Copilot integration

Notebooks will come equipped with data-aware copilot capabilities. Users will be able to use magic commands to generate explanations and code. Code shortcuts will help with the common tasks such as bug fixes and documentation.

VSCode.dev

In addition to the current VS Code integration, users will also be able to work with VS Code in a fully remote mode, with code automatically syncing back to the service.

CI/CD integration

Users will be able to commit all their data engineering artifacts to a git repo and leverage deployment pipelines for deploying items between dev, test and prod.

Microsoft Fabric SDK

Users will be able to work with Data engineering items programmatically thanks to APIs and the Fabric SDK. We will also support the Livy endpoint for programmatic batch job submission.

SYNAPSE DATA SCIENCE IN MICROSOFT FABRIC

Data science is a powerful tool for unlocking the value of data in any organization's analytics workflow. Through the use of data science, organizations can make more informed decisions and gain predictive insights that would otherwise be unattainable.

Today, we are thrilled to announce the preview of the new Synapse Data Science experience in Microsoft Fabric! With data science in Microsoft Fabric, you can utilize the power of machine learning features to seamlessly enrich data as part of your data and analytics workflows.

WHAT IS MICROSOFT FABRIC

Microsoft Fabric is our next generation data platform for analytics and integrates Power BI, Data Factory, and the next generation of Synapse experiences, exposing easy to use analytics experiences for a variety of roles. This unified platform allows users to securely share data, code, models, and experiments across the team and simplifies many aspects of data science from data ingestion to serving predictive insights.

VALUE OF DATA SCIENCE INTEGRATED IN THE ANALYTICS WORKFLOW

Synapse Data Science in Microsoft Fabric allows data science practitioners to work seamlessly on top of the same secured and governed data that has been prepared by data engineering teams. This eliminates the need to copy data and figure out ways to give your data science teams secure access to data. In Microsoft Fabric, the open Delta Lake support allows data science users to version datasets to create reproducible machine learning code. Additionally, data science users have access to a wide range of easy-to-use getting started experiences, low-code tools and code authoring experiences with Notebooks and Visual Studio Code. Synapse Data Science in Microsoft Fabric also provides a rich set of built-in ML tools. For example, MLFlow model and experiment tracking, powered by Azure machine learning, is built in. The SynapseML Spark library provides scalable ML tools and users can serve predictions swiftly to Power BI with the new PBI Direct Lake capability. Finally, streamlined collaboration across different analytics roles makes hand-offs seamless and teams more productive.

Next, we will cover how Microsoft Fabric provides users with a variety of features to help complete end-to-end data science workflows.

DATA SCIENCE FOR BUSINESS INSIGHTS

Problem Formulation And Ideation

The process starts with formulating a question, Collaboration across multiple roles is required for answering these questions. This step is aided by easy access to the same source of truth, such as business metrics, logic, and data analysis tools. Semantic link is a new feature we are launching that will drastically simplify handoffs and ease collaboration between data scientists and stakeholders.

Data discovery and pre-processing

Data engineering teams will build Lakehouses that data scientists can consume. Data scientists will need to further pre-process data to solve problems with ML tools. We are adding a new tool called Data Wrangler to help boost productivity during this tedious step.

Experiment and build ML models

For building ML models, we allow users to create and track ML experiments and models using MLFlow. Users can leverage library management and build environments using third party libraries for developing ML solutions, and the rich SynapseML Spark library that we own and maintain enables model training and ML feature construction to be done at large scale.

Enrich and operationalize

Finally, to enrich and operationalize data with predictive models, data science users can schedule their batch prediction scripts and leverage our scalable PREDICT function to speed up the process. Multiple options exist for operationalization of batch scoring. For example users can leverage a lightweight scheduling of Notebooks to run on a regular basis or schedule Spark jobs that run as part of data pipeline steps.

Gain insights

With the PBI Direct Lake mode, access to predicted values in Lakehouse tables is seamless without the need to load data. Your BI reports will have automatic access to the latest enriched data to help accelerate your predictive business insights!

Through a combination of various well integrated experiences available to a wide range of analytics roles, Microsoft Fabric enables users to successfully complete their data science projects end-to-end.

WHAT'S INCLUDED IN SYNAPSE DATA SCIENCE?

Now that you hopefully have a better understanding of how Microsoft Fabric helps to better integrate data science with analytics and BI, let's take a closer look at some of the new features and experiences we are introducing.

Data prep and code generation with Data Wrangler

Data Wrangler, a powerful, intuitive tool for data wrangling and preparation. Data Wrangler makes data cleansing and preparation easier than ever before, while still allowing users to take advantage of the power of coding and reproducibility of Python. The dynamic data display, built-in statistics and chart-rendering capabilities along with the ability to get started with Pandas data in just a few clicks, make this tool easily accessible to a range of experience levels, from novice developers to seasoned professionals. Future updates will include support for Spark and a natural language processing "to code" functionality via Azure OpenAI.

ML models and experiments as first-class citizens with MLFlow

We are also making machine learning models and experiments first-class citizens in Fabric. Built-in support for ML models and experiments allows users to manage models and track experiment runs using standard MLFLow APIs. Comparison experiences make it easy to compare different experiment runs and auto logging helps capture key metrics automatically as users author code to train models. The Microsoft Fabric MLFlow tracking store is powered by Azure Machine Learning, which opens the possibility of valuable integrated experiences in the future.

SynapseML, a comprehensive machine learning library for Spark

Additionally, we bring you the Synapse ML Library, the richest machine learning library for Spark, owned and maintained by Microsoft. With the goal to simplify distributed and scalable machine learning, this library provides access to many different ML tools and easy to use APIs for applying ML and enriching data at scale. Core capabilities include distributed ML with performant and popular algorithms like LightGBM as well as full MlFlow support for SynapseML models. Spark operators help users to work with pre-trained AI models from Azure Cognitive Services, including the new Azure Open AI features, for applying foundation model powered transformations directly on data with Spark.

Enrich data in your Lakehouse with scalable PREDICT

We facilitate the operationalization of ML models with the scalable PREDICT function for distributed batch scoring on Spark, allowing users to process predictions without moving any data. Users can write the enriched data to the Lakehouse and serve it seamlessly to BI reports with the powerful Power BI Direct Lake capability. Additionally, we introduce an easy-to-use guided experience that helps users quickly and easily generate code to apply their ML models.

R Language support

We understand that many users depend on code authoring with R. That is why we also bring you native support for the R language on Apache Spark. Both through notebook and Spark Job definitions, users can author and run code with SparkR and SparklyR. Library management capabilities for R allow installation of R libraries incl. Tidyverse, so that data scientists can use familiar Spark and R interfaces to process data and develop machine learning models. We hope you enjoy the added flexibility of using R with Apache Spark in Microsoft Fabric.

Going forward, we plan to release many more valuable experiences to help you build data science solutions as part of your analytics workflows. There is a long list of upcoming features and experiences to be aware of. Here are some highlights on our roadmap.

Upcoming features and experiences

Semantic Link (Preview)

Semantic Link offers a powerful set of tools to bridge data science and BI. With Semantic Link, data science users can tap into the semantic data model using familiar tools like Python and Spark. This helps to gain a good understanding of the data and the problem to solve. Analysts and business users that define the semantic model, key measures and business logic can now be confident that data science users will be able to tap into the same source of truth. This drastically improves the collaboration across roles and avoids duplication of effort. Additionally, Semantic Link also helps to validate data and detect data quality issues. Sign up for the private preview for early access and use Semantic Link to explore Power BI datasets from Python and Spark, read measures and measure definitions, and detect data quality issues.

Hyperparameter tuning and AutoML (Preview)

Hyperparameter tuning and AutoML will allow users to automate the process of optimizing machine learning models with the flexibility of FLAML. This process can also be easily tuned to SparkML and SynapseML models and is further supported by code-first integration to parallelize AutoML trials with Spark. Additionally, costs can be reduced by parallelizing hyperparameter trials with Spark, and MLFLow can be used to automatically capture hyperparameter metrics and parameters. All of this is designed to make it easier to build machine learning models.

Pre-trained AI models (Coming soon in preview)

Azure Cognitive Services pretrained AI models will be integrated into Microsoft Fabric, allowing users to access Text Analytics,

Anomaly Detection, Text Translator, and other AI models incl. foundation models from Azure open AI, out of the box without pre-provisioning any resources in Azure. This makes it seamless to apply AI powered transformations on data in Lakehouses.

Copilot experiences in Notebooks (Coming soon in preview)

Developers in Microsoft Fabric will also get a wide array of built-in Copilot experiences that boost developer productivity across the entire analytics workflow. For example, these experiences help notebook users to generate, explain and document code but also trouble shooting and migration assistance. Through integration with best of breed foundation models from Azure Open AI, the Microsoft Fabric Copilot experiences will be contextualized and relevant to the data the user has access to. Stay tuned for more details about these upcoming experiences!

SYNAPSE DATA WAREHOUSE IN MICROSOFT FABRIC

In today's data-driven world, data warehousing is a critical component of any business strategy. Its goal is to assist companies in effectively managing and analyzing vast amounts of data, enabling them to make informed decisions and drive growth. However, with the ever-increasing amount of data being collected, the challenges associated with its management are also growing and this is compounded by the evolution of the era of AI. Traditional data warehousing solutions have become complex and costly, often resulting in data duplication, vendor lock-ins and governance issues.

We are thrilled to announce the preview of Synapse Data Warehouse in Microsoft Fabric! Synapse Data Warehouse is the next generation of data warehousing in Microsoft Fabric that is the first transactional data warehouse to natively support an open data format enabling IT teams, data engineers and business users to collaborate seamlessly and extract actionable insights from their data, all without compromising enterprise security or governance. Just like the previous data warehouse generation, SQL provides multi-table ACID transactional guarantees. It is built on the well-established SQL Server Query Optimizer and

79

Distributed Query Processing engine but is bolstered with the key improvements below that add significant new value to enterprises.

Fully managed: this new data warehouse is a fully managed SaaS solution and effortlessly extends modern data architectures to both professional developers who love to write code and citizen enthusiasts with no coding skills. What previously took enterprises months to accomplish can now be done in minutes efficiently.

No provisioning and managing of resources: instead of provisioning dedicated clusters, it is based on a fully serverless compute infrastructure where resources are provisioned in milliseconds as jobs requests come in. Enterprises benefit from resource efficiencies and only pay for what they use.

Separation of storage and compute: compute nodes used are independent of storage enabling enterprises to scale and pay for either one separately.

Open data standards: data is not locked-in the proprietary SQL Server format but is stored in the open data standard of Delta-Parquet in the Microsoft OneLake providing interoperability not only with all workloads in Fabric but also the Spark ecosystem without requiring any data movement.

Cross-querying: as a result of the open data standard support, data in the lake whether processed by a Fabric workload or any other compute engine can be queried and cross-joined without making any copies of the data.

Auto-scaling: it automatically scales resources instantly as query and usage requirements increase and down-scales when there is no more need for these resources, all without any user intervention.

Self-optimizing: it automatically detects and isolates workloads to deliver predictable performance. The best performance is based on caching which is automatic and multi-tiered based on activity. Query plans generated are optimal. There is no need to hire highly skilled engineers to manage workload groups or tune the data warehouse.

Fully integrated: it is fully integrated with all Fabric workloads right out of the box for any developer. Users can continue to benefit from the rich capabilities of the SQL engine using the T-SQL language or a simple user interface. All this with the continued benefits of the SQL ecosystem.

Let's dive deeper into its capabilities.

Analytics is a continuum of activities requiring the ability to ingest, prep and analyze data, creating business semantics, machine learning models and BI reports. It requires collaboration across IT, data engineers, business analysts and data scientists across the organization. As data is shared or discovered, it needs to be secured and governed. Synapse Data Warehouse makes this easy through the key capabilities below.

Simple and intuitive Warehouse experience

Fabric has a dedicated home page for data warehouse, where a new Warehouse can be created with just a name and sensitivity label. There's no provisioning or setup required. The user interface is a familiar relational database experience. The Warehouse Explorer exposes schemas, tables, stored procedures, and all other database objects. Anyone new to warehousing can start with a Warehouse sample!

Easily ingest and prep data

Data can be loaded into the Warehouse writing T-SQL queries using the COPY command. It can also be ingested using a Data Factory Pipeline which is available now or Dataflow Gen2 which will be available soon, from right within the Warehouse Editor. Pipelines offer connectivity to several data sources, ability to sub-select tables and preview data. Tables are automatically created, and column data types are automatically mapped from source type to Parquet. Data ingested into the Warehouse is stored in OneLake. Table transactions are guaranteed by the SQL compute engine and Delta logs are published periodically. Delta-Parquet in OneLake can be viewed using OneLake Explorer and accessed effortlessly using Notebooks.

Analyze data visually or by writing code

The professional developer can continue writing T-SQL code for querying and analyzing data. Citizen developers can use the Visual Query Editor which is a drag-and-drop user interface for compiling queries and even performing complex joins and groupings. T-SQL is automatically generated, which can be edited as well.

Virtual warehouses for cross-joining warehouses and lakehouses

Traditionally, when users wanted to merge data from both the data warehouse and the lake, they were faced with a cumbersome process of creating pipelines, transferring data, and duplicating their data. In Microsoft Fabric, users can create virtual warehouses containing data from any source in Fabric whether a Warehouse or Lakehouse and across any storage or any cloud. As long as the data is in Delta tables, a shortcut can be created to it and queried or cross-joined using T-SQL three-part-naming conventions or the Visual Query Editor.

Add business semantics to data and build Power BI reports that serve insights

Synapse Data Warehouse is fully integrated with Power BI in Microsoft Fabric. A Power BI dataset is automatically generated and kept in sync with the data in the Warehouse. Users do not have to worry about Power BI modes and make trade-offs based on their data volumes increasing or needing to meet performance or security requirements. The experiences to create relationships between tables, add Power BI semantics known as measures is all within the Warehouse Editor. A new Power BI report is a one-click experience!

Manage security and govern data

Data warehouse supports traditional T-SQL security constructs. GRANTS, REVOKE or DENY can be used to secure objects with the Warehouse. Object level security allows for controlling granular access for both collaboration and consumption.

Data governance is critical for enterprises. Like the rest of Microsoft Fabric experiences, sensitivity labels can be applied to the Warehouse which carries forward to any item downstream. End-to-end lineage information can be viewed as well.

Performance and scale

Data Warehousing in Microsoft Fabric is currently in preview. The focus of this preview is on providing a rich set of SaaS features and functionality tailored to all skill levels. The preview delivers on the promise of providing simplified experiences through an open data format over a single copy of data. While this release is not focused on performance, concurrency, and scale, additional functionality to handle complex workloads and provide industry-leading performance will land incrementally as we progress towards General Availability of data warehousing in Microsoft Fabric.

Azure Synapse Dedicated SQL Pools update

Existing Azure Synapse Dedicated SQL Pools will continue to provide a robust, enterprise-grade PaaS solution. Synapse Data Warehouse in Microsoft Fabric is an evolution in the form of a simplified SaaS solution that can connect to the existing PaaS offering. Customers will be able to upgrade from their current products into Fabric at their own pace.

COMING SOON

In addition to what is shipping at preview, rich capabilities will be released every month and details updated via monthly blog posts. Here are just a few features to give you a sneak peek:

Automatic statistics

statistics are automatically computed in the Warehouse as queries are executed ensuring users get optimal performance.

Zero copy Table clones

users can create zero copy Table clones using a T-SQL command.

Data warehouse in Deployment Pipelines

users can use Warehouses in Deployment Pipelines and deploy to Dev, Test and Production workspaces. They can compare schemas, rollback changes and automate via the use of REST APIs.

Data warehouse Git integration

users can connect to a Git repository, develop their warehouse SQL scripts and code, manage versions, commits, and pull requests and download SQL projects.

Data warehouse REST APIs

users can use public REST APIs to automate creation, management, and administration of their data warehouses.

Warehouse integration with Microsoft Fabric Monitoring Hub

users can view query details, monitor, and troubleshoot performance of their solution end-to-end using the Monitoring Hub.

Dataflows Gen2

users can use Dataflows Gen2 with familiar Power Query experiences to transform data and load into the Warehouse.

SENSE, ANALYZE, AND GENERATE INSIGHTS WITH SYNAPSE REAL-TIME ANALYTICS IN MICROSOFT FABRIC

In our personal lives, we've become accustomed to accessing and consuming data in an interactive, on-demand, and easily accessible way. From streaming movies and TV shows to ordering food and groceries online, we expect to have what we need at our fingertips in real-time. This shift in data consumption has been powered by big data, streaming data ingestion, and indexed, keyword-based search, all of which have simplified the user experience. However, many organizations have struggled to keep up with this shift due to the complexity of their data systems and lack of appropriate tools. This is where Synapse Real-Time Analytics in Microsoft Fabric comes in.

With Real-Time Analytics, organizations can simplify their data integration and focus on scaling up their analytics solution while democratizing data for everyone, from citizen data scientists to advanced data engineers. Real-Time Analytics enables quick access to data insights through automatic data streaming, indexing, and partitioning, and employs auto-generated queries and visualizations, all while preserving powerful analytical capabilities. The platform is optimized for streaming, time-series data, and utilizes a query language and engine with exceptional performance for searching structured, semi-structured, and unstructured data.

One of the key advantages of Real-Time Analytics is its seamless integration with all Fabric experiences, including Lakehouse, Data warehouse, Data Integration, and Power BI. This allows organizations to leverage the full power of the Fabric platform to store, manage, process, and analyze their data with ease. Real-Time Analytics can ingest data from any source and in any data format, without the need to build complex data models or create scripts to transform the data. Imported data undergoes default partitioning and indexing, allowing users to work with versatile data structures and query structured, semi-structured, or free text.

Integration With Other Workloads

Another major advantage of Real-Time Analytics is its ability to scale to an unlimited amount of data, from gigabytes to petabytes, with unlimited scalability on concurrent queries and concurrent users. Real-Time Analytics is an ideal solution for businesses that need to work with high-speed, high-volume data streams. It's also well-suited for organizations that require real-time insights to drive their decision-making processes. If you need to ingest data quickly, with high freshness and low query latency, Real-Time Analytics is an excellent choice.

Additionally, if you need to work with structured, semi-structured, or unstructured data formats, including free text, Real-Time Analytics offers the necessary flexibility. With its ability to handle large volumes of data and optimized time-series database structure, Real-Time Analytics is a valuable tool for organizations across a range of industries, including finance, transportation and logistics, smart cities, smart buildings, manufacturing operations, automotive, and oil and gas.

Real-Time Analytics also includes

- Simplified Get Data experience for bringing data from any format and source.
- One-click Power BI report generation.
- One Logical Copy – data can be available to Microsoft OneLake and exposed to other Fabric experiences.
- Truly serverless – no SKU selection.
- Real-time streaming data availability in seconds from ingestion to querying.
- Querying OneLake data via OneLake shortcuts.

- Seamless connectivity with Azure Data Explorer for databases via Cloud Connection.
- Real-time complex data structure transformation.

In summary, Synapse Real-Time Analytics in Microsoft Fabric is a fully managed big data analytics platform that simplifies data integration and democratizes data for organizations. It allows organizations to focus on scaling up their analytics solutions while seamlessly integrating with other Fabric experiences. With its ability to ingest data from any source, query raw data without transformation, and scale to handle massive amounts of data, Real-Time Analytics is a powerful tool for organizations looking to stay ahead in the data-driven world.

MICROSOFT FABRIC AND COPILOT IN MICROSOFT POWER BI

Businesses have been collecting and storing massive amounts of data from apps, services, Internet of Things (IoT) sensors, and other sources for decades. And every year, the volume of data collected grows at staggering rates.

But harnessing value from this data has proved challenging for most. Siloed data gets out of sync. Inconsistent data could lead to high integration costs. Poor data quality sabotages new AI models. Out-of-date reports cause misinterpreted insights. All of this stifles the ability to unlock the full value of data, hampering innovation and AI experiences.

Today, we are excited to unveil Microsoft Fabric and Copilot in Microsoft Power BI. Fabric, now in preview, is an end-to-end, human-centered analytics product that brings together all an organization's data and analytics in one place. It brings together the best of Microsoft Power BI, Azure Synapse, and Azure Data Factory into one unified software as a service (SaaS) platform. Data engineers, data warehousing professionals, data scientists, data analysts, and business users can seamlessly collaborate within Fabric to foster a well-functioning data culture across the organization.

Copilot in Power BI, now in private preview, combines advanced generative AI with your data to help everyone uncover and share insights faster. Simply describe the insights you need or ask a question about your data, and Copilot will analyze and pull the right data into a stunning report—turning data into actionable insights instantly.

What's included in Microsoft Fabric

See Arun Ulagaratchagan's blog post to read the full Microsoft Fabric Preview announcement.

Fabric offers six experiences: a Data Factory-powered data integration experience, Synapse-powered data engineering, data warehouse, data science, and real-time analytics experiences and business intelligence (BI) with Power BI—all hosted on a lake-centric SaaS solution. We are also developing an experience called Data Activator that will help customers respond to changes in their data instantly by setting up a system of detection that automatically alerts the team with the right context to take action.

READ MORE ABOUT EACH OF THESE NEW EXPERIENCES BY READING THE FOLLOWING ANNOUNCEMENT BLOGS

Data Factory announcement blog

With Data Factory in Fabric, organizations can unify their hybrid and multicloud data estates and unlock value with a data integration experience that combines the ease of use of Microsoft Power Query with the scale and power of Data Factory. Currently in preview.

Synapse Data Engineering announcement blog

The next generation of Synapse data engineering in Fabric empowers data engineers with a world-class Spark platform with great authoring experiences that can help transform data at scale and democratize data through the lakehouse while collaborating effectively. Currently in preview.

Synapse Data Warehouse announcement blog

Synapse Data Warehouse provides industry-leading SQL performance and scale. For the first time, data engineering, data warehousing professionals, and BI analysts can operate on a unified open format allowing a single copy of truth for all personas. Currently in preview.

Synapse Data Science announcement blog

Data scientists can work side by side with their data engineering and BI counterparts to build rich AI models at speed and scale. Currently in preview.

Synapse Real-Time Analytics announcement blog

Organizations can use Synapse Real-Time Analytics to explore data and perform real-time analysis on large volumes of data streaming from applications, websites, IoT devices, and more with high performance and low latency. Currently in preview.

Data Activator announcement blog

Data Activator in Fabric enables users to create a system of detection that monitors analytics to drive timely human and automated actions across an organization. Currently in private preview.

OneLake announcement blog

OneLake is the "OneDrive for data." It is a complete, rich, enterprise-wide data lake provided as a SaaS service. OneLake is core to Fabric's lake-centric approach. Currently in preview.

WHAT DOES MICROSOFT FABRIC MEAN FOR POWER BI USERS?

Power BI customers will continue to enjoy all the functionalities that they have available today. With the launch of Fabric, Power BI Premium customers can simply turn on the Fabric tenant setting in the admin portal. With Fabric's unified capacity model, Power BI Premium capacity can be utilized by any of the new workloads. Read this documentation for more information on Fabric's single capacity model. Power BI Pro customers can access this functionality through capacity trials.

Beyond providing access to the six other powerful experiences in Fabric, we are also announcing several Power BI Premium only features designed to transform how you analyze and visualize your data.

NEXT GENERATION OF AI WITH COPILOT IN POWER BI

Introducing Copilot in Power BI! With Copilot in Power BI, we are infusing the power of large language models into Power BI at every layer to help users get more done and create more value from their data. Using Copilot, you can simply describe the visuals and insights you're looking for, and Copilot will do the rest. Users can create and tailor reports in seconds, generate and edit DAX calculations, create narrative summaries, and ask questions about their data, all in conversational language. With the ability to easily tailor the tone, scope, and style of narratives and add them seamlessly within reports, Power BI can also deliver data insights even more impactfully through easy-to-understand text summaries.

We've already released the quick measure suggestions for DAX capability that helps analysts quickly create the code they need. The rest of the Copilot in Power BI experiences are now in private preview. Stay tuned to the Power BI blog for the latest updates and public release date for Copilot in Power BI.

UNIFIED DATA FOUNDATION WITH ONELAKE AND DIRECT LAKE MODE

Power BI is standardizing on open data formats by adopting Delta Lake and Parquet as its native storage format to help you avoid vendor lock-in and reduce data duplication and management. Direct Lake mode unlocks incredible performance directly against OneLake, with no data movement. Combining this with the ability for the other analytical engines to read and write data directly in the lake, Fabric will reshape how business users consume big data. Power BI datasets in Direct Lake mode enjoy query performance on a par with import mode, with the real-time nature of DirectQuery. And the data never leaves the lake, so there is no need to manage refreshes.

We are thrilled to announce the preview of Direct Lake mode for Power BI datasets on Lakehouses. We plan to launch the preview for Direct Lake mode datasets on Data Warehouses soon. For now, Direct Lake mode datasets for Warehouse is in private preview, but it does take effect if you use the SQL Endpoint for Lakehouse.

To try Direct Lake from your Lakehouse or Warehouse in Fabric, click on New Power BI Dataset, select the tables you want to include, and click Confirm. Open the data model to create measures and relationships as you would for any other Power BI dataset. Lastly, click new report and create beautiful Power BI reports. Note the integrated experience from data in the lake through to report creation without leaving the browser or performing a refresh.

ENTERPRISE-GRADE COLLABORATION WITH GIT INTEGRATION FOR POWER BI DATASETS AND REPORTS

We are also enabling more seamless collaboration with your development team on Power BI content with Git integration. You can now easily connect your workspace to Azure DevOps repositories to track changes, revert to previous versions, and merge updates from multiple team members into a single source of truth that will be synced into the workspace with a single click.

As a developer, you can use this integration to:

- Use Power BI Desktop to author report and dataset metadata files in source-control friendly formats.
- Save as a Power BI project (.PBIP) to a folder instead of to a .PBIX file.

- Enable multiple developer collaboration, source control integration to track version history, compare different revisions (diff), and revert to previous versions.
- Use continuous integration and continuous delivery (CI/CD) to enforce quality gates prior to reaching production environments.
- Enable code reviews, automated testing, and automated build to validate the integrity of a deployment.

Users can leverage Git integration and deployment pipelines for an end-to-end application lifecycle management of their work by developing through Git integration and deploying their Power BI content across dev, test, and production workspaces. Developers can use the user interface (UI) experience or automate the process through other tools, such as Azure Pipelines.

END-TO-END GOVERNANCE ACROSS FABRIC

Building analytics solutions is complicated. Data teams must manage everything from user roles to data ingestion, security, compliance, collaboration, workspaces, and more. With Fabric, Power BI, Synapse, and Data Factory are unified on a single unified SaaS platform. This allows data teams to collaborate in a single workspace, on the same copy of data, with centralized administration, governance, and compliance tools. These capabilities include data lineage and impact analysis, data protection with sensitivity labels, data endorsement, admin monitoring, and more. And these unified experiences make it easy to jump between tools and collaborate with others on the team. Moreover, with the large amount of data and analytical projects being built within an organization, efficient discovery and management is key. The OneLake Data Hub empowers everyone in the organization to centrally discover and explore data available to them and relevant to their business domain, take further action, or build upon what others have started.

Universal compute capacities simplify purchasing and managing analytics projects

Purchasing and managing resources is massively simplified with Fabric. Customers can purchase a single pool of compute that powers all Fabric experiences. With this all-inclusive approach, customers can create solutions that leverage all workloads freely without any friction in their experience or commerce. The universal compute capacities significantly reduce costs, as any unused compute capacity in one workload can be utilized by any of the workloads. For Power BI Premium customers, existing Power BI Premium P SKUs will automatically support all the new Fabric experiences. Starting June 1, new Fabric SKUs will be available for purchase in the Azure portal that give you access to all these experiences.

HOW DO I GET STARTED WITH MICROSOFT FABRIC

Enabling Fabric in your Power BI tenant

Power BI customers can get access to Fabric today by turning on the Fabric tenant setting in the Power BI admin portal. To give Power BI administrators time to prepare, we have turned off the switch by default. You can choose to opt in or out of Fabric through the admin portal. You can also choose to enable Fabric for specific users or security groups within your tenant. If no action is taken by the administrator, Fabric will be turned on by default for all Power BI tenants starting on July 1.

Additionally, if you would like to try Fabric in one or more capacities before enabling it for the entire tenant, it can be enabled for specific capacities in the capacity settings tab within the admin portal. Like the tenant setting, this capacity setting can also be limited to specific users or security groups.

Upgrading existing Power BI Premium capacities

If your administrator has turned on Fabric at the tenant level, all Premium capacities will automatically be upgraded to support Fabric. In addition, capacity administrators can turn on Fabric at the capacity level (as described in the previous section), allowing anyone with access to this capacity to use the new Fabric experiences. To help you prepare for how this will impact your usage of Power BI Premium, new Fabric experiences will not draw down usage from your capacity before August 1, 2023. You can, however, monitor how Fabric impacts your capacity usage through the Capacity Metrics app.

Universal Fabric capacity is free to try for 60 days

If you do not yet have Power BI Premium, you can get access to a free Fabric trial (learn more about the Fabric trial). If trials are enabled by your tenant administrator, you will automatically be granted a Fabric trial capacity when you (1) create an item that requires a capacity or (2) click on Start trial from your account manager in the upper right-hand side of the portal.

This capacity can be used with one or more workspaces, allowing you to create data warehouses, lakehouses, notebooks, and more.

After 60 days, you can purchase Fabric Capacities in the Azure portal (available after June 1).

And as a tenant admin, you will have visibility into all active trial capacities provisioned for users within the tenant in the Power BI admin portal.

Fabric learning resources

To help you get started with Fabric, there are several resources we recommend:

- Microsoft Fabric learning paths: Experience a high-level tour of Fabric and how to get started.
- Microsoft Fabric tutorials: Get detailed tutorials with a step-by-step guide on how to create an end-to-end solution in Fabric. These tutorials focus on a few different common patterns including a lakehouse architecture, data warehouse architecture, real-time analytics, and data science projects.
- Microsoft Fabric documentation: Read Fabric docs to see detailed documentation for all aspects of Fabric.

DRIVING ACTIONS FROM YOUR DATA WITH DATA ACTIVATOR

Your data is only valuable if you can act on it. This means you need to generate insights from your data, then convert those insights into jobs to be done. If you are like many organizations, you meet this need today by manually monitoring a set of reports and dashboards. This can be time-consuming, and that time is multiplied across each department, region, and business unit in your organization.

You can reduce the time involved through automated monitoring but, to date, automation has typically required writing code. Coding can be expensive and brittle, and the costs involved mean that few organizations have found it worthwhile to invest in automation.

That is why we have envisioned a brand-new way to act on your data. We call it Data Activator. Data Activator is a no-code Microsoft Fabric experience that empowers the business analyst to drive actions automatically from your data.

PUTTING DATA ACTIVATOR TO USE

Data Activator can act on any type of data in Microsoft Fabric, from relatively slow-moving data in warehouses, to real-time

106

streaming data in Azure Event Hubs. Here are a few examples of how you might put Data Activator to use in your organization:

Sales

alert a sales manager if a particular customer is in arrears with their payments

Inventory

check whether inventory levels for a particular product are sufficient, and notify an operations manager if not.

IT Operations

automatically monitor data quality metrics and kick off remedial processes if those metrics are below target.

IoT

automatically create an engineering support ticket if a refrigerator temperature is too high.

HOW DATA ACTIVATOR WORKS

Data Activator drives actions through a 3-step process:

Connect to your data

Data Activator can connect to a wide range of data sources in Microsoft Fabric, from Power BI datasets, Eventstreams, and more. Once Data Activator is connected to your data, it continually monitors it for actionable patterns.

Detect actionable conditions

Data Activator gives you a single place to define actionable patterns in your data. These can range from simple thresholds (such as a value being exceeded) to more complex patterns over time (such a value trending down).

Trigger actions

When Data Activator detects an actionable pattern, it triggers an action. That action can be an email or a Teams alert to the relevant person in your organization. It can also be triggering an automatic process, via a Power Automate flow or an action in one of your organization's line-of-business apps.

Get started with Data Activator

You can create a Data Activator trigger directly from within Power BI. Just click a visual, then choose "trigger action" to create an alert on that visual's data. For real-time streaming data, just point Data Activator at your Event Hub.

Designing Triggers

Data Activator's trigger designer lets you define trigger conditions with a visual, no-code tool. Here, a trigger sends a Teams notification if a machine on the factory floor is vibrating too much:

Sign up for the Data Activator preview!

Data Activator is currently in preview. To get the preview, first get Microsoft Fabric (see below for details). Then, sign up for the Data Activator preview at aka.ms/dataActivatorPreview. We would love to hear from you!

ADMINISTRATION, SECURITY AND GOVERNANCE IN MICROSOFT FABRIC

We are excited to announce the preview of Microsoft Fabric. Fabric provides a unified intelligent data foundation for all analytics workloads and integrates Power BI, Data Factory, and the next generation of Synapse to offer customers an easy to manage, modern analytics solution.

While each of these experiences may cater to different personas pursuing specific tasks like a data integration engineer building a pipeline for data ingestion, a data scientist fine-tuning an ML experiment or a BI professional creating a Power BI report, they will all coexist within a single SaaS-ified product experience reducing the need for integration and facilitating better collaboration.

In addition to the intuitive and familiar experience, these Fabric experiences are unified through a common foundation which includes Microsoft OneLake that ensures one copy of your data, breaking data silos, AI capabilities which help accelerate productivity and discover insights with your data but most importantly industry leading capabilities that make Fabric Secure and Governed by default.

As more and more data is made accessible for analytics, along with it comes the risk of oversharing or unintended use of business-critical data. In Fabric we will provide you visibility into what is happening in your tenant, equip you with insights into usage and adoption and provide key capabilities to secure and govern your data end to end. Microsoft Fabric also provides built-in enterprise grade governance and compliance capabilities, powered by Microsoft Purview.

Centralized Administration

The Fabric Admin portal equips administrators with tenant-wide governance and empowers them to centrally manage, review, and apply configurations for their tenants and capacities. As a tenant admin, you can set security configurations for your entire tenant, so every data engineer or data scientist need not worry about it.

In addition to that, Capacity Settings provides you visibility and allows you to manage all capacities in your tenant including the newly introduced Fabric capacities. Tenant admins will also have visibility into all active Fabric trial capacities provisioned for users within the tenant. Similarly, as a capacity admin, you will be able to manage all capacities you are an admin of (including your own trial capacity).

Enabling Microsoft Fabric in your tenant

Fabric admins can control availability of Fabric preview workloads for users within your tenant using the Fabric tenant setting in the admin portal. To give Power BI administrators time to prepare, we have turned off the switch by default. You can choose to opt in or out of Fabric through the admin portal. You can also choose to enable Fabric for specific users or security groups withing your tenant. If no action is taken by the administrator, Microsoft Fabric will be turned on by default for all Power BI tenants starting on July 1, 2023.

Additionally, if customers would like to try Microsoft Fabric in one or more capacities before enabling it for the entire tenant, it can be enabled for specific capacities in the capacity settings tab within the admin portal. Like the tenant setting, this capacity setting can also be limited to specific users or security groups.

Admin Monitoring and Capacity Insights

As admins, to effectively govern, we understand that you need insights into usage, adoption, and activities within your tenant. Hence, we introduced the admin monitoring feature which is an in-product admin monitoring workspace with pre-created reports and datasets. This feature will soon extend to include Fabric artifacts and additional governance capabilities like who has access to what, unused artifacts and more.

Capacity Metrics provides Admins with insights from all Premium capacities so they can easily monitor performance of workloads and make data-driven capacity scale up decisions. Telemetry from all Fabric workloads along with the SaaS platform is delivered in a single set of turnkey analytics.

The utilization graph shows the amount of capacity that has been consumed compared to the amount that has been purchased based on SKU size or allocated via Trial. Aggregate views let users identify resource usage trends across workloads and operations and their impact to autoscale & throttling decisions by the SaaS platform. Drill-through experiences let users zoom into understanding detailed usage telemetry with full fidelity to enable performance optimization.

During the Fabric preview, Trial Capacities can run both preview and production workloads. The Metrics App shows both in one place so Admins can plan for capacity scale-up with confidence using data from their own organizations' usage patterns.

Fabric governed and compliant with Microsoft Purview

Fabric governed and compliant with Microsoft Purview is deeply integrated into Fabric, providing enterprises with scalable governance and compliance capabilities, with the benefit of natively being built into the Fabric platform. These capabilities include sensitivity labels that persist as data flows from the lakehouse through Fabric and to Office, automatic detection of sensitive data through data loss prevention policies, end to end auditing and in near future will include Purview data catalog as well.

Microsoft Purview data catalog will empower users to easily browse and search for specific Fabric data assets. One of the significant advantages of the Purview-Fabric integration is that it will eliminate the need for additional Purview RBAC (Role-Based Access Control) configuration to discover Fabric artifacts in Microsoft Purview data catalog. The simplified user experience and reduced administrative overhead will allow organizations to quickly unlock the value of their data. Additionally, you will be able to annotate and curate Fabric data assets in Purview data catalog. With just a few clicks, users will be able to add descriptions, terms, tags, or other relevant metadata to enrich the information associated with a particular artifact. The additional business and technical context associated with Fabric artifact will enhance data understanding, promote collaboration, and improve the overall data governance practices within an organization.

Integration with Microsoft Purview Information Protection sensitivity labels brings into Fabric the well-known concept of sensitivity from Office, where you can see if the document or email is confidential, and you may not be authorized to export sensitive data. This is all done through Information Protection sensitivity labels, and these very same sensitivity labels are integrated into Fabric. When a data owner applies a sensitivity label to a lakehouse or any other Fabric item, the label will flow with the data to all downstream items in Fabric. Moreover, when exporting data from Fabric to Office files, the label and protection settings will automatically be applied to the Office files.

In addition to the above, Fabric admins can gain valuable insights into Fabric's data estate with Fabric's Microsoft Purview Hub (preview), which is available within the Fabric experience. Microsoft Purview Hub contains insights about sensitive data, certified and promoted items, and a gateway to advanced capabilities in Microsoft Purview portals.

Compliance admins can use Microsoft Purview Data loss prevention (DLP) policies to define DLP policies to detect the upload of sensitive data (such as social security number) to Power BI models in Fabric. If such an upload is detected, the policies will trigger automatic policy tip visible to data owners in Fabric and can also trigger an alert for compliance admins. DLP policies can automate the compliance processes to meet enterprise-scale compliance and regulatory requirements in an effective way.

Finally, Fabric is also integrated with Microsoft Purview audit which provides Fabric and compliance admins with end-to-end auditability of Fabric activities. All user and system operations are captured to the audit logs and made available in Microsoft Purview compliance portal.

Lineage, Endorsement and Metadata scanning

Lineage and Impact analysis in Fabric

In modern business intelligence projects, understanding the flow of data from the data source to its destination can be a challenge. The challenge is even bigger if your team has built advanced analytical projects spanning multiple data sources, processes, data items and reports. Fabric data lineage and impact analysis helps you answer questions like "What happens if I change this data?" or "Why isn't this report up to date?" and more. With Fabric data lineage and impact analysis, you can easily track the flow of your data from source to destination and understand how it impacts your business. This powerful tool helps you make informed decisions about your data and ensures that your reports are always up-to-date.

Certify and promote your Fabric items (Endorsement)

Organizations often have large amounts of data and processes available for sharing and reuse by their Fabric users, and identifying the trustworthy, authoritative items can be challenging. With Endorsement, items which should serve as sources of truth, or are recommended, can be marked accordingly, making it easier for users to find the high-quality data they need. Once content is endorsed, it is clearly labeled and receives priority across the various Fabric experiences, or in Analytic solutions when connecting to Fabric data (such Power BI Desktop). Thus, enabling more efficient, trustworthy creation, and better decision making.

Tenant metadata scanning

With the massive amounts of emerging data, it is key for administrators to gain visibility on the data artifacts being created and managed in their organizations. To that extent, Fabric introduces metadata scanning capabilities, in the set of Admin REST APIs (known as scanner APIs), enabling administrators to efficiently and automatically retrieve valuable information about their organization's Fabric assets, such as inventory, metadata, and lineage. In turn, they can leverage this information for their own custom-made solutions and insights.

Enterprise promises – Security and more...

Securing your data is a non-negotiable priority for us. For your Fabric data stored at rest in your home region, or in one of your capacities possibly at a remote region of your choice, we ensure that data never leaves the region boundary and is compliant with data residency requirements We also support E2E auditability for Fabric, so all Fabric user and system operations are captured in audit logs and made available in Microsoft Purview.

For access control, the existing Power BI workspace roles now extend to cover Fabric artifacts as well with additional permissions which are specific to new Fabric artifacts. In addition to workspace roles, you will be able to share individual Fabric artifacts or provide direct access to them to specific users very soon.

OneLake is automatically provisioned for every Fabric tenant, and it provides out-of-the-box governance such as data lineage, data protection, certification, catalog integration, etc. All data is ultimately under the control of a tenant admin. Additionally domains allow for federated governance providing granular control by business area.

MICROSOFT ONELAKE IN FABRIC, THE ONEDRIVE FOR DATA

Organizations invest heavily in data lake strategies with the vision of having a central place to store all their data, break down silos, and simplify data blending, analysis, security, governance, and discovery.

In reality, the vision is highly illusive. Enterprise data lakes are mostly implemented as custom projects using raw storage covered with massive glue code designed to enable scalability, collaboration, compliance, security and governance. Data mesh patterns with independent business domain-driven lakes adds additional overhead and fragmentation with multiple teams managing their own siloed lake resources. To break down these silos, these organizations build additional complicated solutions with complex data movement to facilitate sharing and reuse. And for all this to become usable for the business side, IT organizations must also build data warehouses, data marts, and cubes creating additional copies the lake data. The resulting data lake implementation is often a complex and hard to manage system, rife with both siloes and redundant data.

INTRODUCING MICROSOFT ONELAKE

Introducing Microsoft OneLake – "the OneDrive for Data". OneLake is a complete, rich, ready-to-go enterprise-wide data lake provided as a SaaS service. Just like organizations are using OneDrive for their documents, they now have OneLake for their data. OneLake is the core of Fabric's lake-centric approach. It provides customers with:

- One data lake for the entire organization at scale
- One copy of data for use across multiple analytical engines
- One security model living natively with the data in the lake (coming soon)
- A centralized OneLake data hub for data discovery and management

One data lake for the entire organization

OneLake improves collaboration over a single organization wide data lake. Each Fabric tenant will have exactly one OneLake where all the data of all the projects and for all the users will be stored. OneLake is automatically available with every Fabric tenant with no additional resources to setup or manage.

121

Governed by default with distributed ownership for collaboration

The concept of a tenant is a unique benefit of a SaaS service. It establishes clear governance and compliance boundaries controlled by the tenant admin and all data in OneLake is governed by the tenant policies. This well-controlled system allows OneLake to be open to every user to add their own contributions to OneLake from every part of the organization without any friction.

Just like every Office user can create a new Teams channel or SharePoint site without coordinating with the admin, OneLake enables similar distributed ownership through workspaces. Workspaces enable different parts of the organization to work independently while all building the same data lake. Each workspace has its own administrator and access control. Each workspace is powered by a capacity that resides in a user selected region. This means that OneLake fully accommodates customers doing business in multiple countries and natively supports local data residency requirements. OneLake spans the globe with different workspaces residing in different countries while still remaining part of the same logical lake.

Data mesh and domains

With Microsoft OneLake, we provide a unified data lake that eliminates all data silos. However, the capabilities extend further. OneLake also provides the ability to organize and manage data in a logical way allowing different business groups to efficiently operate and control their own data. This pattern is known as "data mesh".

With Onelake native support for data mesh, organizations can easily define business domains, such as Marketing, Sales, Human resources, and more. Once domains are defined and contain the respective OneLake data, various consumption, and governance capabilities light-up for the domain. This allows more optimized consumption for business users, and more granular control per domain for administrators.

For example, data owners and businesses can discover and consume Onelake data filtered to their areas of interest, and administrators can delegate settings to the domain level, allowing different definitions and governance per business unit.

With the built-in OneLake domains, OneLake is the first data lake that provides native support for data mesh as a service.

Open at every level

OneLake is open at every level. Built on top of Azure Data Lake Storage Gen2, OneLake can support any type of file, structured or unstructured. All Fabric data items like data warehouses and lakehouses will automatically store their data in OneLake in delta parquet format. This enables data engineers to load a lakehouse using Spark, SQL developers to load data in fully transactional data warehouses using T-SQL, and all contributors to build the same data lake.

OneLake supports the same ADLS Gen2 APIs and SDKs to be compatible with existing ADLS Gen2 applications including Azure Databricks. Data in OneLake can be addressed as if it were one big ADLS storage account for the entire organization. Every Fabric Workspace appears as container within that storage account while different data items appear as folders under those containers.

OneLake file explorer for Windows

OneLake servs as the OneDrive for data. Just like OneDrive, OneLake data is easily accessed from Windows using the OneLake file explorer for Windows. In Windows, you can navigate all your workspaces, data items, easily upload, download or modify files just like you can do in OneDrive. The OneLake file explorer simplifies data lakes making them accessible to even non-technical business users.

One copy of data

OneLake aims to give you the maximum value out of a single copy of data without data movement or duplication. You will no longer need to copy data just to use it with another engine, or to break down silos so that data can be analyzed with other data.

Shortcuts let you connect data across business domains without data movement

A large organization will typically have lots of data domains with different data owners. Shortcuts provide connections between different data items across domains so that data can be virtualized into a single data product without data duplication, data movement, or changing the ownership of the data.

A shortcut is a symbolic link. It functions as metadata that points from one data location to another. They are similar to Windows shortcuts. When you create a shortcut from one location to another location, files will appear in the shortcut location as if they physically exist. Tables in a warehouse can be made available to another lakehouse without copying the data from the warehouse to the lakehouse. Since all the data is already in OneLake, you can just create a shortcut from the warehouse to the lakehouse and the data will appear in the lakehouse as if you had copied it. Because the data isn't copied, there is no secondary copy to maintain. When data changes in the warehouse, those changes are automatically reflected in the lakehouse.

Shortcuts are used to consolidate data across workspaces and domains without changing the data ownership. The same data can be used multiple times across different locations while the original owner remains responsible for loading and managing it.

Shortcuts to Azure Data Lake Store gen2

Organizations already have their data in lakes outside of OneLake. We have extended shortcuts to also support these data stores. You can create shortcuts to existing ADLS gen2 accounts enabling all your data to be virtualized into OneLake and the data appears as if it physically exists. The owners of these accounts can continue to manage them independently of OneLake.

Shortcuts to S3 make OneLake the first multi-cloud data lake

OneLake goes beyond Microsoft and Azure to become the first multi-cloud data lake with shortcuts to Amazon S3 buckets. Through shortcuts, S3 buckets can be virtualized into OneLake. Their data is mapped to the same unified namespace and can be accessed using the same APIs including the ADLS gen 2 APIs. Notebooks, SQL queries and Power BI reports can all span multiple clouds without the end users needing to be aware that they are doing so. Transparent smart caching (coming soon) will bring data closer to compute and reduce egress costs.

Shortcuts to Dataverse (coming soon)

Dataverse generates shortcuts to Microsoft Fabric, generates Synapse Lakehouse and a SQL endpoint for Dynamics 365 and PowerApps data enabling next generation Power BI capabilities. This direct integration between Dataverse and Microsoft Fabric eliminates the need to build and maintain custom ETL pipelines or use third party data integration tools. Dataverse shortcuts ensure that data always remains within Dataverse and as data gets updated in Dynamics 365, changes are reflected in Power BI reports automatically.

Data analysts will be able to launch Microsoft Fabric directly from the PowerApps experience. Data engineers can launch Microsoft Fabric using Synapse Link and work with data using Python or Spark notebooks. Direct integration between Dataverse and Microsoft Fabric saves significant time and effort.

One copy of data with multiple analytical engines

Compute powers all the analytical experiences in Fabric. With OneLake in Fabric, compute is completely separate from storage. While OneLake represents the one data store for the entire organization, Fabric's other multiple analytical computes can access the same copy of data without needing to import it into another copy. There is no longer a need to copy data just to use it with another engine. You are always able to choose the best engine for the job that you are trying to do.

For example, imagine you have a team of SQL engineers building a fully transaction data warehouse. They can use the T-SQL engine and all the power of T-SQL to create tables, transform, and load data to tables. If a data scientist wants to make use of this data, they no longer need to go through a special Spark/SQL driver. All the data is stored in OneLake in delta parquet format.

Data scientists can use the full power of the Spark engine and its open-source libraries directly over the data.

Business users can build Power BI reports directly on top of OneLake using the new Direct Lake mode in the Analysis Services engine. The Analysis Services engine is what powers Power BI Datasets and has always offered two modes of accessing data, import and direct query. Direct Lake mode gives users all the speed of import without needing to copy the data, combining the best of import and direct query.

If you have a data engineering team which prefers to use Spark to build a lakehouse, they can use notebooks to land their data in OneLake in delta/parquet format. That data can be consumed automatically by all engines. The same is true for data that is landed using other engines using the ADLS DFS APIs, or virtually added through shortcuts. When defining your organization's data strategy, you no longer need to optimize for different teams with different skillsets and preferences. Teams that want to work with SQL, can work with SQL. Teams that want to work with Spark, can work with Spark. Teams using other engines to land their data, can continue to do that. Everyone builds the same data lake. There are no silos.

One security model (coming soon)

Managing data security (table, column, and row levels) across different data engines is a persistent nightmare for customers. OneLake will bring with it a universal security model enabling you to define security definitions just once. Unlike other solutions which require you to define security definitions in some other layer, these security definitions will live in OneLake alongside the data. Security definitions will be enforced uniformly across all engines inside and outside of Fabric. This model is coming soon.

OneLake data hub

Lastly, OneLake has provided a central solution for all data, however how can this data be accessed, discovered, managed, reused? These aspects are key as organizations increasingly require easy access and discovery of high-quality data for reuse, decision-making and data-driven insights. We're excited to introduce the OneLake data hub (an evolution of the Power BI data hub). The OneLake data hub serves as a centralized interface to all data housed within OneLake, including data warehouses, lakehouses and their SQL endpoints, KQL databases, datamarts, and datasets. OneLake data hub is the central location for easy data discovery, data management, and data reuse.

With the OneLake data hub users can see data across their business domains and filter to see a specific domain that they are interested in, see all authoritative endorsed data in one place and see all the data owned by users to make data management easy as possible in one central location.

The OneLake data hub is particularly powerful for users who have access to data across multiple workspaces. The OneLake data hub explorer offers an intuitive and efficient means of browsing through workspaces in order to locate specific data items. With the explorer, users can more quickly and easily access large volumes of data.

Once data is discovered, users can perform a large variety of actions: explore its properties and tables, identify whether it is marked as sensitive and should be treated with caution, track data lineage and perform impact analysis across workspaces, reuse that data and build on top, find valuable insights and make informed business decisions, or take further action.

The OneLake data hub is integrated into multiple experiences within both Fabric service and Power BI Desktop. This integration ensures that users can quickly and easily find necessary data in any context and in a consistent manner. For instance, in Power BI Desktop, users may access the OneLake data hub experience to browse available items and connect with them, thus avoiding the need to create new data sources. This approach fosters a culture of data reusability and helps organizations meet their goals more effectively.

INGEST, TRANSFORM, AND ROUTE REAL-TIME EVENTS WITH MICROSOFT FABRIC EVENT STREAMS

You can now ingest, capture, transform and route real-time events to various destinations in Microsoft Fabric with a no-code experience using Microsoft Fabric event streams. It enables customers to ingest real-time event data from external event sources into the data stores in Fabric. The events could be transformed into the native formats required for target destination. For example, Eventstream could transform the events into Delta Lake format for the Lakehouse, into SQL columns based on the table schema, or filter events so that homogenous data can be sent to a KQL table.

To create a new instance of Microsoft Fabric event streams, navigate to Real-time Analytics in your Fabric workspace where you will find Eventstream.

After creating a new Eventstream item, you will land into a no code & easy to use experience where you can configure your eventstream from source to destination.

WHAT IS FABRIC EVENT STREAMS

Centralized place for real-time events

It provides the capability to capture, modify, and direct your streaming data in real-time using a fully managed and scalable infrastructure.

Multiple source connectors

It enables you to ingest your real-time streaming data from 3 source types today: Azure Event Hubs, Sample data or Custom application.

Multiple destinations

It enables you to transform/capture/route real-time streaming data to 3 destination types today: KQL database, Lakehouse, or Custom application.

No code experience

It provides an intuitive and easy to use drag & drop experience with end-to-end data visibility and monitoring.

Let's dive into each point stated above in detail:

1. Centralized place for real-time events

Microsoft Fabric event streams utilize a scalable infrastructure that efficiently manages scaling and resourcing automatically. This enables you to effortlessly capture your real-time events, facilitating streaming ETL (Extract, Transform, Load) operations, as well as transforming and routing the events to your desired destination.

2. Multiple source connectors

Microsoft Fabric event streams enable you to ingest your real-time event data from 3 source types today:

- Azure Event Hubs: You can seamlessly ingest events from an Azure event hub configured using Fabric Data connections.
- Sample data: You can easily configure your eventstream to continuously ingest sample events from either Yellow Taxi data or Stock Market data.
- Custom application: With this source, a streaming endpoint is created that allows customers to have their custom streaming application communicate directly with Fabric with either a Kafka client or an AMQP client.

3. Multiple destinations

Microsoft Fabric event streams enable you to transform and/or route your real-time event data to 3 destination types today:

- Fabric KQL Database: This destination helps with direct ingestion of your real-time events into KQL database. Once the data lands in KQL database, you can then perform additional queries/analysis to gain deeper insights or build Power BI reports.

- Fabric Lakehouse: With this destination, you can transform (manipulate, filter, aggregate etc.) your real-time events before routing into a Lakehouse table. Real-time events are converted into Delta Lake format and then stored in the designated Lakehouse tables.

- Custom application: With this destination, you can configure your custom applications to use their Kafka or AMQP client application to pull the events directly from Fabric.

4. No code experience

There is a super simple & easy to use drag & drop experience with end-to-end data visibility. You can view the shape of your data at every step from source to transformation to destination. You can also monitor each step by looking at meaningful insights.

MICROSOFT 365 DATA + MICROSOFT FABRIC BETTER TOGETHER

Microsoft Graph is the gateway to data and intelligence in Microsoft 365. It provides a unified model to access the tremendous amount of data in Microsoft 365 including Teams, Outlook, SharePoint, Viva Insights, and more. Use the wealth of data in Microsoft Graph to build forward looking business insights to unlock insights on customer relationships, business processes, security and compliance, and people productivity.

Now you can bring all your Microsoft 365 data into Microsoft Fabric. Microsoft 365 Data Integration for Microsoft Fabric is a feature of the new Microsoft Fabric solution, which enables you to manage your Microsoft 365 alongside your other data sources in one place with a suite of analytical experiences that seamlessly work together to transform your data into competitive advantage. Microsoft Fabric includes Data Factory, Data Engineering, Data Warehousing, Real-Time Analytics, Data Science, and Power BI, all hosted on a lake-centric SaaS solution for simplicity and to maintain a single source of truth. Learn more about Fabric.

Access all your Microsoft 365 data though Microsoft Graph Data Connect

To access your Micrsoft 365 in the Microsoft Graph for enterprise analytics, we use Microsoft Graph Data Connect which a secure, scalable solution that enables you to copy relevant Microsoft 365 datasets into Microsoft Fabric.

Microsoft 365 datasets comes ready for analysis. **We deliver data in three formats: basic, cleaned, and curated.**

- Basic datasets: Datasets generated from raw customer created content and inputs from M365 Applications and Services

- Cleaned datasets: Datasets generated by either normalization and de-duplication from Basic Datasets. Or datasets created from user activity or behavior signals in M365.

- Curated datasets: Datasets custom generated for a specific use case or analytics scenarios. Or datasets from 1P M365 analytics application for their extensibility.

DATA ENGINEERS EXTEND EXISTING DATA MODELS WITH MICROSOFT 365 DATA

Getting started is easy! In Fabric, once you've created a data pipeline, you'll see the copy assistant with the new Microsoft 365 connector (shown in the diagram below). Simply click to set up your link to Microsoft 365 through Microsoft Graph Data Connect. Once your connection is configured, you can then choose and select the dataset that you want to bring into Fabric. Then, with just a few clicks, your Microsoft 365 data appears in OneLake in the analytics-ready delta parquet format.

Once you open OneLake from your workspace, you now can immediately see the copied Microsoft 365 data and leverage all the analytics tools available in Fabric to generate insights. Plus, you're also taking advantage of the enterprise governance and security that helps protect all data in Fabric.

DATA ANALYSTS BUILD ACTIONABLE ENTERPRISE ANALYTICS WITH MICROSOFT 365 DATA

Once your Microsoft 365 data is in Microsoft Fabric OneLake, you can construct use cases empowered by Microsoft 365 data from Power BI. Insights built from Microsoft 365 data come from passive network analysis, as compared to self-reported surveys, measure interactions through existing email and meeting data resulting in minimal missing data, less upfront investment, and reduced time burden. This also means that you can access all your historic Microsoft data for use cases including:

Information Oversharing is a security and compliance use case powered by our newly available SharePoint usage and activity (ODSP) dataset. This allows customers to better understand how Microsoft Information Protection (MIP) labels are constantly protecting SharePoint data, maintain information boundaries, and establish new rules based on how sensitive data is managed and classified. To learn more about Information Oversharing, watch an on-demand webinar: M365 Data + Synapse Webinar

Organizational Network Analysis (ONA) is a structured way to visualize how communications occur within the organization. Organizational Network Analysis harness information flows and team connectivity to unlock productivity, innovation, employee engagement, and organizational change. This can be useful in a wide variety of network related insights to:

- Measure the effectiveness of an agile transformation progress or enablement session. Conversely, detect post-merger integration or post-reorg issues.
- Reduce management escalations with the strategic introduction of shared services.
- Accelerate time to new hire integration (onboarding) by identifying gaps in shared learning to drive cross organizational learnings and best practices.
- Promote diversity and inclusion in the workplace by uncovering demographic imbalances.

Matthew Matteucci, Professor, Department of Electronic Information and Bioengineering, Politecnico di Milano notes that "Customers will better understand their human capital. From there, they can reduce stressors or react to other factors that prompt people to seek other employment— that's our ultimate goal."

MICROSOFT GRAPH DATA CONNECT NOW AVAILABLE IN 14 REGIONS

Microsoft Graph Data Connect is now enabled in 14 regions (nine new regions since January 2023). The following table indicates which Microsoft 365 regions are supported and the corresponding Azure regions required for data movement (see below). Click here to learn more about enabled regions.

Cross Geography Access Updates: Currently, tenants with multi-geo capability enabled in Microsoft 365 (link) can only access Microsoft Graph Data Connect datasets in their respective geographic location. This means that data across multiple regions need to be manually joined together to prepare for analysis, which can often be a slow, error-prone process. With this update, we remove that limitation for companies with multi-geo tenants.

However, to maintain stringent data residency requirements, we have intentionally scoped this only for directory related datasets: Azure Active Directory (see here) and Microsoft Groups (see here). These datasets enable users to run system metadata analysis including our Information Oversharing use case.

ENHANCED SECURITY WITH MICROSOFT GRAPH DATA CONNECT

Microsoft Graph Data Connect is a highly secure, governed, and privacy centric environment that ensures your sensitive PII data is secure through every step of the process. We are continuing to build enhanced security capabilities.

We are announcing support for Azure Managed VNet-Integration Runtime through Mapping Data Flows in Azure Data Factory and Azure Synapse Analytics. To connect from Azure today, whether you're in Azure Synapse or Azure Data Factory, there needs to be a service in Azure that talks with the Microsoft Graph Data Connect service.

Integration Runtime (IR) is an Azure powered service used by Azure Data Factory and Azure Synapse Analytics pipelines to provide data integration capabilities across different network environments. Microsoft Graph Data Connect customers leverage this feature to ensure a secure data flow between Azure and Microsoft 365 services to the customer's destination storage account.

Managed V-net IR with Mapping Data Flows allows customers to better protect their sensitive data by ensuring communication only happens through their private and protected network. This

143

capability aims to improve network level security during data egress within Microsoft Graph Data Connect by connecting to a private VPN with secure credentials. This new capability allows for a simplified security set up as customers no longer need to use the public internet for data transit and can set up their private endpoints to ensure more secure, end-to-end data movement.

Microsoft Graph Data Connect now supports Managed v–net IR as a security feature to meet the needs of customers in highly regulated industries that care deeply about secure data storage, encryption, and isolation.

EXTENSIVE JOINT SOLUTION ECOSYSTEM

Microsoft Graph Data Connect has collaborated with a rich network of enterprise technology vendors who have built powerful, joint solutions on Microsoft 365 data:

Microsoft 365 Data Integrations

Microsoft Graph Data Connect is natively integrated to many Azure services. Here are some that are now available:

- M365 Data + Microsoft Fabric (Preview)

- M365 Data + Azure Synapse Analytics (Generally Available)

- M365 Data + Azure Data Factory (Generally Available)

NEW DATAVERSE ENHANCEMENTS AND AI-POWERED PRODUCTIVITY WITH MICROSOFT 365 COPILOT

At Microsoft Build 2023, we're announcing new AI, low code, and data management capabilities that enable our Dynamics 365 customers to complete time-consuming tasks faster and gain more insights from their business data. We're also introducing enhancements to Dataverse, our smart, secure, scalable, low-code data platform that 97% of Fortune 500 companies rely on. Together, these updates make it easier than ever for organizations to extend their Dynamics 365 enterprise applications and business processes across the Microsoft Cloud securely and compliantly.

UNLOCK AI-ENHANCED PRODUCTIVITY WITH YOUR DYNAMICS 365 DATA

Two months ago, we announced Microsoft 365 Copilot, a revolutionary new way of working that uses AI to enable users to get answers and perform tasks using natural language prompts. Available now to early access customers, Copilot combines the power of a large language model, Microsoft productivity and business apps, and your data—your calendar, emails, chats, documents, meetings, and contacts—to do things you've never been able to do before, just by telling it what you want. For example, give Copilot a natural language prompt like "Tell my team how we updated the product strategy," and it generates a status update based on the morning's meetings, emails, and chat threads.

We're excited to announce that now Microsoft 365 Copilot can incorporate your Dynamics 365 and Power Platform data stored in Dataverse, all in an easy-to-use, unified experience. By replacing dozens of steps in multiple apps and constant context switching with simple, natural language prompts, imagine what your teams can accomplish in minutes instead of hours:

A sales professional can generate a status update for the top 25 leads based on engagement activity over the past two weeks.

A marketer can summarize topics and needs from responses and update an email marketing campaign in real-time.

A customer service manager can summarize the top trending customer issues from the past week as an email to senior leadership.

Microsoft 365 Copilot automatically inherits the native security and governance framework of Dataverse and applies user security and permissions at runtime.

DYNAMICS 365 AND MICROSOFT FABRIC, BETTER TOGETHER THROUGH DATAVERSE

Organizations want to make better decisions that are based on data. Dataverse integrates Dynamics 365 business application data with Microsoft tools that deliver actionable insights and reporting, like the Dataverse Power Query connector, rich Dataverse integrations with Power BI, and Azure Synapse Link for Dataverse.

Today at Build, Microsoft announced Microsoft Fabric, a new, end-to-end analytics platform. Data Factory, Data Engineering, Data Warehousing, Real-Time Analytics, Data Science, Data Activator, and Power BI are all hosted on a lake-centric SaaS solution for simplicity and to maintain a single source of truth. This makes your business data more easily discoverable and accessible, so that you can use it to make better decisions every day.

Today we're also happy to announce "View in Microsoft Fabric" for Dataverse. Coming later this year to every Dynamics 365 customer, "View in Microsoft Fabric" automatically makes all your Dynamics 365 data available for analysis in Microsoft Fabric without having to copy data, build ETL pipelines, or use third-party integration tools. With just one click, you'll get more insights from your business data stored in Dataverse.

Your Dynamics 365 data doesn't leave the Dataverse governance boundary. Changes are reflected in Power BI reports automatically. Dataverse also automatically generates an enterprise-ready Synapse Lakehouse and SQL endpoint for your Dynamics 365 data in Microsoft Fabric. This makes it easier for data engineers and DB admins to combine data from multiple sources and build custom analytics in Spark, Python, or SQL.

ELIMINATE DATA SILOES WITH FABRIC AND DYNAMICS 365

Microsoft Fabric's lake-centric approach helps to eliminate data silos. Combine data from your applications and devices—web sites, mobile apps, sensors, and signals from your warehouse and factories—with data from your business processes in Dynamics 365—sales, cases, inventory, and orders—to predict potential delays or shortages that affect keeping your promises to customers.

Direct integration between Dataverse and Microsoft Fabric saves significant time and effort. Your makers can build low-code apps and automations to orchestrate business processes and react to insights found in Microsoft Fabric using connectors to over 1,000 apps. Add those insights back to Dataverse as external or virtual tables through the SQL endpoint and makers can turn them into low-code apps with Power Apps, Power Pages, or Power Automate using skills they already have.

OPTIMIZE YOUR CAPACITY COSTS WITH LONG-TERM RETENTION POLICIES IN DATAVERSE

The longer an enterprise application runs, the more historical data it accumulates. Often, customers must keep this data to comply with compliance and regulatory requirements, but storage costs mount up. With the new long-term retention capability in Microsoft Dataverse, you can save on storing inactive data that's rarely accessed without investing in custom archival solutions.

From the Power Apps maker portal, admins can set retention policies with criteria driven by compliance requirements and manage the policies with a dashboard. The retained data has security controls and governance applied and never leaves your Dataverse environment. Admins can access it when needed using advanced find. No new data or security model is required, even if you later customize the application or Dataverse tables.

Admins can view the impact of data retention policies in Power Platform admin center capacity reports, which show the retained capacity and associated savings.

NEW ZERO-TRUST SECURITY FEATURES IN DATAVERSE

The foundation of any enterprise-grade solution is security. Dataverse enables even more granular security in Dynamics 365 and Power Platform with new IP access management and managed encryption key features.

IP enforcement

As organizations continue to adopt and build solutions in Dataverse, it's increasingly important to restrict access to data to the right users at the right times and places. Govern user access in real-time with Azure Active Directory (Azure AD) continuous access evaluation IP restrictions and an IP firewall.

- IP restrictions. Azure AD access evaluation restricts unauthorized access based on IP address by evaluating user-critical events like account deletion. When changes that require restriction of user access occur, access is denied in near–real-time.
- IP firewall. Azure AD puts valuable business data behind an IP firewall that can restrict user access if the IP address isn't a part of a trusted network. Threats like insider data exfiltration or token replay attacks can be mitigated for all business processes running in Dataverse.

ENCRYPTION KEYS

In addition to improving granular security access, Dataverse safeguards sensitive customer data by integrating Azure Key Vault customer-managed encryption keys ("bring your own key") in Dataverse environments. Organizations can create a Power Platform enterprise policy that can be applied to individual or groups of Dynamics 365 and Power Platform environments across storage types like analytics, logs, and more.

Dataverse is the data platform supporting Dynamics 365, and we're committed to delivering the advancements your organization needs to support and scale to any enterprise application.

CONCLUSION

Microsoft Fabric is a platform that allows users to get, create, share, and visualize data using various tools. To share content and collaborate in Microsoft Fabric, your organization needs to have an organizational license and at least one individual license.

A Microsoft Fabric subscription consists of tenants, capacities, and workspaces and can be organized in various ways according to your organizational needs.

Microsoft Fabric is an all-in-one analytics solution for enterprises that covers everything from data movement to data science, Real-Time Analytics, and business intelligence. It offers a comprehensive suite of services, including data lake, data engineering, and data integration, all in one place.

With Fabric, you don't need to piece together different services from multiple vendors. Instead, you can enjoy a highly integrated, end-to-end, and easy-to-use product that is designed to simplify your analytics needs.

The platform is built on a foundation of Software as a Service (SaaS), which takes simplicity and integration to a whole new level.

Microsoft Fabric is a prerelease online service that is currently in public preview and may be substantially modified before it's released. Preview online service products and features aren't complete but are made available on a preview basis so that customers can get early access and provide feedback.

Printed in Great Britain
by Amazon